THE
SEVERED
SOUL

THE SEVERED SOUL

A PSYCHOANALYST'S HEROIC BATTLE TO HEAL THE MIND OF A SCHIZOPHRENIC

DR. HERBERT S. STREAN

AND

LUCY FREEMAN

ST. MARTIN'S PRESS
NEW YORK

DESIGN BY DIANE STEVENSON / SNAP·HAUS GRAPHICS

Library of Congress Cataloging-in-Publication Data

Strean, Herbert S.
    The severed soul : a psychoanalyst's heroic battle to heal the mind of a schizophrenic / Herbert Strean and Lucy Freeman.
        p.   cm.
    ISBN 0-312-03930-1
    1. Schizophrenics—Case studies.   2. Psychotherapist and patient—Case studies.   I. Freeman, Lucy.   II. Title.
RC514.S8253   1990
616.89′82′092—dc20   89-24344

First Edition

10 9 8 7 6 5 4 3 2 1

This book is dedicated to Nancy W. and all those who suffer as she did.

Easy is the descent to Avernus
Night and day the door of dark Hades lies open
But to retrace your step
To escape to the upper airs
This is the task, this is the labor.

Virgil, Aeneid, *VI, 126–129*

CONTENTS

Acknowledgments   xi
Prologue   xiii

PART I

THE FIRST YEAR
Spring 1980

1
Lost in a Mental Haze   5

2
The Smouldering Rage   19

3
The Sound of Anger   43

4
The Sexual Explosion   77

PART II

THE SECOND YEAR
Spring 1981

5
An Unforgettable Death   103

6
The Little Princess   125

CONTENTS

PART III

THE THIRD YEAR

Spring 1982

7

Growing Up Too Swiftly   155

8

Who's Got the Power?   177

PART IV

THE FOURTH YEAR

Spring 1983

9

Dreams That Unlock Psychic
Torture   205

10

The Murder Within   225

PART V

THE FIFTH YEAR

Spring 1984

11

The Courage to Go It Alone   257

EPILOGUE

More Human Than Otherwise   285

ACKNOWLEDGMENTS

The authors wish to thank, first and foremost, Robert Weil, senior editor, for his many valuable suggestions, his sensitive editing and his awareness of the importance of psychoanalytic help for those who have difficulty coping with their conflicts. We also thank Bill Thomas, assistant editor, for his important contributions and Jon Gertner, editorial assistant.

We express our gratitude to Sharyn Rosenblum, for her work as publicist at St. Martin's Press and for suggesting the book's title, as well as her spirited championing of its message. Thanks also to Raquel Jaramillo for her eloquent artistry that produced the dramatic jacket.

Our thanks also go to Jane Dystel, our literary agent, who believed in the theme of the book. We are fortunate, too, in having Marcia Strean's suggestions along the way. Last, but not least, we are grateful to Nancy Winthrop, a pseudonym for the real heroine, an extremely aware and intelligent woman, who permitted us to use her story so others might benefit.

Dr. Herbert S. Strean
Lucy Freeman

PROLOGUE

She sat on the hard hospital bed, attacking a sheet of white paper. The words formed as she scribbled away, desperately trying to make sense out of chaos.

Putting words on paper had always calmed her, even as a little girl. The verbal exercise made her feel less tortured. She wrote:

A city of red brick set in green hills,
I cry for my sanity,
Not more madness in this palace of the crazed.

She put down the pencil, stared around at the bare, cracked walls. It was a peeling room—like her soul, exposed, bleeding. She was a prisoner in this barren jail with its wooden dresser, skewed drawers containing her hairbrush, cotton nightgown, another set of panties, brassiere, pocketbook, comb and brush.

She stood up, stared at her face in the dresser mirror. People told her she looked somewhat like a wan Marilyn Monroe. Pale blue eyes stared back at her. Sometimes she had to look in the mirror just to make sure she was still alive—or force herself to cry just to feel the luxury of an emotion.

Suddenly the door opened—no knock, no warning. In walked the tall, mustached, white-uniformed doctor. He made her think of a cadaver, so emotionless was his nasal voice. He stared at her as though she were a cretin.

Beside him strode his plump ally, also in white, the nurse.

They were nameless, just puppets to her, as she was to them. There was no courtesy of, "May I come into your private room?", only invasion by the enemy.

This was an enemy that always brought hurt in some way. A pill that triggered pain in the stomach and head. An electric shock as she lay bound on a metal table that pulverized her body and spirit. Or, sometimes, the dreaded needle that injected a shot of some strange medicine into her buttocks. That fiery jolt, to her, was the final torture.

She felt like a guinea pig in a chamber of horrors. She wasn't worth a smile, or a "How do you feel today, Mrs. Nancy Winthrop?" She would have liked to hear her full name once in a while to distinguish her from her fellow prisoners.

She felt constantly attacked in this hospital. The doctor had recently told her, "You're a brilliant woman. You've got a college degree and you've even been a graduate student. You should be able to get your life in order, don't you think?"

She wanted to reply, You bastard, if I knew how to do that I wouldn't be here in this stinking hellhole, would I? You are supposed to tell me how to become a happy woman—one who doesn't want to die but to live.

And now that doctor was walking over to her with his little black bag, the one with the needle and the medicine in it. She started to shudder and shiver. She backed away from his cold, steely eyes.

He put the bag down at the foot of the bed, opened it slowly, meticulously, as though it held half a million dollars. He drew out the needle and a little brown bottle. He said patronizingly, "You'll feel better after this." Then he lowered the needle into the bottle, gathered what she thought was the poison that made her feel even more out of the real world.

She begged in a low voice, "Please don't do this to me. It hurts too much. I will die. You're slowly trying to kill me, aren't you?" And then, pleading, "I can't fight back. You have all the power."

He walked close to her, needle in hand. She started to moan, "Please, please, please." Then she screamed, no longer able to control the deep fear that spread through her mind and body, "Get away from me, you murderer! Leave me alone! I hate you! Hate you! Hate you!"

He said in that unctuous voice, "Come on, now. You're making a fuss over nothing. This won't hurt. We're here to help you."

He turned to the bovine nurse and ordered, "Get her ready."

She knew he really meant, "Pull up the hospital gown, take off her panties, expose her buttocks, place her facedown on the bed."

A scene flashed into her mind from childhood when her father had inflicted the same pain, sometimes in the same place. She screamed again, "No! No! No!", tried to fight off the nurse who had arms like a prizefighter.

It was then she gave up, as she always had given up, allowed the nurse to pull up her gown, pull down her panties, expose her bare buttocks, place her facedown on the white pillow.

Again the doctor's voice, "This won't hurt."

Her final entreaty: "It always hurts a lot. Can't you stop

assaulting me with that needle?" The pleas of her lifetime. Then, a whisper, "I'm afraid I will die."

The doctor now sounded stern. "Just relax, please, Mrs. Winthrop. I don't have all day."

She mustered the courage for one last plea. Her voice rose in a subdued scream. "You must stop this torture!"

Suddenly there was anger in his voice. He barked, "And you have to stop this useless fighting. We only want you to get well."

He grabbed a fleshy part of her left buttock, plunged in the needle.

She could not help herself, she shrieked, "It hurts! It hurts! You're a bastard! I'm going to report you. I cannot stand any more of your violence and hate. This hospital is full of hate. The nurses hate us. The doctors hate us. Isn't it enough that we hate ourselves?"

She turned over, outraged at being once more the victim, not entitled to a plea, screamed, "All I want is to be left alone! Stop trying to murder me! You are all killers."

The doctor told the nurse, "Put restraints on her hands and legs and see that she stays in bed the rest of the day. Feed her, but that's all. And lock the door when you leave. I want her in isolation, I don't want her stirring up the other patients."

The nurse tied her hands, she would not be able to write poetry anymore that day. Then tied her feet, she could not even walk to the bathroom. She felt like a prisoner of the Nazis. And what was her crime? She did not know.

The doctor left first, without even saying good-bye, followed by the nurse, who locked the door. She had become their complete captive.

She had once again tried in vain to avoid the plunge of the needle. This was violation of a woman's most private right. It was like a violent rape. Bloody rape.

The tears started in a trickle, then coursed down her cheeks. She sobbed, cried out to an empty room, "Is there no one who will help me? Oh, God, must I always be alone in a sea of enemies?"

She longed for someone to comfort her, take her in his arms, hold her close. Say to her softly, "I love you, dear Nancy, I will see that you never suffer again. I will take care of you, cherish you forever."

But the room, like her life, was empty. The door was locked so she could not escape.

She was once again in that familiar hostile world. She felt truly desperate. She had to discover a way out, a more compassionate way to help her cope with her agony.

P A R

T   I

THE
FIRST
YEAR

SPRING
1980

1
LOST
IN A
MENTAL
HAZE

**April
1980**

I opened the front door to my office and faced a woman who could have been beautiful if her expression had not been tinged with sadness. She looked as if she wished to unleash tears of years past.

Her features were delicately chiseled, a perfect nose, firm lips, large blue eyes that stared squarely into mine. Dark brown hair curled to her neck. She was rather slight, about five feet two inches, stood tentatively on heels almost two inches high.

Her simple black crepe dress fell to her knees, she carried a matching black silk purse. Even her stockings were black, as though she were on her way to a funeral, not her first analytic session. Perhaps she believed analysis was a death of sorts, as some patients do, I thought.

"Please come in, Mrs. Winthrop," I said.

She had called for an appointment, saying, "I teach second grade in an elementary school. I have heard you speak at psychology meetings and have read three of your books. I would like a consultation about an unruly child in my class who refuses to study or obey me."

She stood stiffly before me like a marble madonna, as if afraid to make another move into the room where I spend as much time as I do at home with my wife. It is a comfortable room, a quiet room, designed to relax the patient, yet it is cheerful too, with windows facing north to catch the morning sun, unless I draw the beige drapes so the patient can concentrate on his internal world. The drapes at each side, from ceiling to floor, hide five shelves stacked with psychoanalytic journals.

My office is on the fifth floor of a building in New York City near Central Park West in the nineties. Only the First Church of Christian Science rises between the park and me. At the time of Nancy's appearance, the park was a colorful palette of reds, oranges, yellows, and greens.

Mrs. Winthrop silently surveyed what she undoubtedly thought was my lair. She saw, in front of the windows, my desk, holding a number of photographs of those important in my life. My wife and our two sons, now postgraduate students. Reuben Fine, founder of the New York Center for Psychoanalytic Training, of which I am now director. My father, Lyon P. Strean, Ph.D., a bacteriologist, and my uncle, George J. Strean, M.D., obstetrician and gynecologist (I grew up thinking "labor" was a town, so often did I hear him say, "There's a woman in labor I have to see").

On the righthand side of the room stand two chairs and a round table that holds a large expressionistic sculpture, *Mother and Child*, appropriate décor for analytic treatment, I had thought, as I bought it. The mother, of black marble, and the baby, of white marble, are entwined. Two chairs, one on either side of the table, I use to supervise analytic students or for the occasional patient who needs to sit up, instead of lying on the couch across the room. Over the table hang three prints of Paris, bought by my wife when we visited that city, which add color to the white walls.

The couch stretches against the opposite wall, facing the windows. Beside it, within easy reach of the patient, stands a small table bearing tissues to stem the many tears that are an inevitable outcome in the analysis of man or woman. A second table between the back of the couch and my green leather chair and hassock holds a telephone and answering machine.

On my wall in clear view is my doctoral degree from Columbia University and a certificate from the Society for Psychoanalytic Training. All patients should make sure their analyst is qualified. Behind my chair is the door through which patients enter.

On either side of the door stand floor-to-ceiling shelves

filled with psychoanalytic books. Atop one bookcase is a photograph of Dr. Theodor Reik, founder of the National Psychological Association for Psychoanalysis. I received psychoanalytic training at this Institute after graduating in 1953 from Boston University's School of Social Work. Both Freud and Reik, at least in spirit, are my constant companions in this room where I work long hours, often well into the evening. A photograph of Freud hangs on the wall next to the couch.

All this Nancy Winthrop could have seen as she stepped into the room. But she seemed unaware of her surroundings, as are many patients when they first enter. Sometimes it takes months before they comment about a picture on the wall or my credentials.

Nancy made no attempt to walk farther into the room, as though it held the horrors of hell. Instead, she stood silently at the door.

I gestured toward the two chairs to our right and asked, "Will you sit here?"

She walked the few steps to one chair slowly, as though to her own execution. Then she lowered herself reluctantly into it. I took the other chair, between us the sculpture of *Mother and Child*.

I waited for Nancy to speak, she had said not one word, wanting me to lead the way. She just stared at me with those blue eyes. If they ever gain some semblance of emotion, they might be very expressive, I thought.

I broke the silence. "How can I help you?"

I sighed with relief as I heard her say, like a plaintive child, "There's an eight-year-old boy in my class driving me mad. He will not accept discipline. He throws violent temper tantrums when anyone asks him to do the simplest task, like writing a letter to a friend."

Over the years I have learned—and even hold as an axiom—that when anyone, but particularly a parent or teacher, complains about a child's behavior, he reveals his own feelings, as though he were guilty of the act about which he complains. The fastest way to find out how an adult pictures himself is to ask more details about the child who has upset him.

So I inquired, "Why do you think this boy gets so angry at your trying to discipline him?"

With her first show of emotion, she said, "I know he really wants to be a one-year-old. He yearns to be a baby. He can't accept the responsibility of being eight. He wishes to be king of the universe, as when he was born."

She added with vehemence, "I *hate* kids who demand so much. They have to learn to accept limits."

By describing this unruly eight-year-old boy, Nancy was telling me, without being aware of it, that *she* felt like a rebellious child who wanted what she wanted when she wanted it. *She* wished to be queen of the realm, resented anyone who tried to dethrone her. *She* was emotionally entrapped in the conflicts and fantasies of her early life. I felt almost joyous that she was so articulate. It would make our work easier.

Nancy quickly changed the subject. Her voice was now almost harsh. "My reason for coming here, Dr. Strean, is not really the boy in my class. I blame him but it's actually the school's principal."

She stopped. I looked at her, my eyes questioning, waited for her to go on.

She obliged me with a rush of words, "The principal is the one out to get me. When I walk in each morning he stares at me with murder in his eyes, as if he wishes I were dead and gone. And he's in cahoots with the rest of the faculty."

Another thing I had learned early in my career is that, however wild or outlandish a patient's complaint, the therapist must accept it as if it were real, even though the complaint may indeed be imagined. Otherwise the patient senses the therapist's skepticism, feels rejected and misunderstood. I experienced several emotions as I listened to what sounded very much like Nancy's fictional charges. I felt discomfort realizing that a paranoid woman was raving in my office. Most of my patients were not this emotionally ill. I also felt compassion, knowing her inner pain must be intense.

Acting as though she were telling the truth, even helping to embellish her fantasy, I asked, "How long have they all been after you?"

She gave a sigh, relieved that I seemed to accept and understand her accusations. Then with a half-smile, she said, "I'm so glad you asked me that. You're a good detective, Doctor. I became aware that they all hated me about three weeks ago when eight-year-old David acted provocatively. I told him to stay after school because he'd misbehaved and then the whole mob—the principal and faculty—marked me for murder."

"For disciplining a child?" I could not help sounding surprised.

"Yes, Doctor. They accused me of being unnecessarily angry at David, of trying to hurt him. But that's what *they* wanted to do to David. And to me."

She explained further, "You're a psychoanalyst, you know what projection is. They really hate David, but can't accept their hatred for a child, so they hate me."

As Nancy spoke of the "mob" and their "hatred" for her, I felt quite sure that it was she who had projected her hatred onto them. I knew it would take months before she would feel safe enough with me to acknowledge her own deeply buried anger at those who had hurt her as a child.

Nancy also had to protect herself against the panic aroused by the fantasy of carrying out a murderous rage against her early attackers. She achieved this by making herself the victim of fantasied murderers. Thus she did not have to feel so terrified of the wish to commit murder or of her deep guilt at such a wish. In the mind of every child, and in the unconscious of every adult, the wish appears the same as the deed and guilt lies heavy on the heart.

The main feeling of an analyst toward a patient is not sympathy but empathy—the belief in the patient and the wish to understand the complexity of emotions and fantasies within that have caused torment. The analyst does not just tolerate but actually encourages anger within a patient, empathizes with his wish to murder, to get revenge for past wrongs, real and imagined.

There were moments, I admit, when it was difficult to feel empathy for the depressed, selfish, me-first attitude of the schizophrenic person. But I always encouraged him to speak on. I never gave medication for I do not believe in drugs as a psychoanalytic tool.

As I understood Nancy more, I was less apprehensive and felt I could come gradually to accept her plight. I was tempted at times to act like a father with a panic-stricken little girl who needed protection from a hostile world. I was flooded with memories of when I was nine years old and taking care of my "baby sister." As Nancy spoke of how she felt "bullied" by the principal and faculty, I recalled moments I had defended and protected my sister from neighborhood bullies.

While few psychoanalysts have described in print how they feel when treating a patient, I have found it is often the subjective reaction, such as the one I produced about my sister, that influences the analyst's thoughts. Visualizing Nancy as my baby sister helped me feel like a protective big brother who wished to take care of her. But this feeling had to be monitored, for Nancy was my patient, not my sister. I admonished myself, You are not a member of Nancy's family but her psychoanalyst who will try to help her face her hidden fantasies so she can move more into the world of reality.

There was no doubt Nancy was clearly feeling "bullied," despite the fact she was projecting her own bullying wishes onto others. I had to respect her way of arming herself mentally by using the common defense of projection. I needed to find out more about her enemies and why they wanted to destroy her.

"Why do you think the principal and faculty want you out of the way?" I asked.

She explained simply, as though to the village idiot, "These people are very frightened of their murderous wishes toward children and they resent me because I have mine under control. They envy me, they're very childish, Dr. Strean."

She added with a sigh, "Every morning the principal looks at me with great hostility as I walk into school. He resents my adult maturity. That is why he is plotting to poison my soup at lunch—and trying to persuade his faculty to harass me!"

Again Nancy was telling me something of her buried self as she talked of her persecutors. She was clearly the one who wished to murder others for what they had done to her, or what she *imagined* they had done.

As she continued to talk of her tormentors, I perceived Nancy as a little girl telling a make-believe story and enjoying the fantasy. Several times during the consultation I felt as if I were engaged in play-therapy with a child. Together we seemed to be making up stories about avengers. As often happens when two people are emotionally in sync, she validated what I experienced.

She said with gratitude, "It's a wonderful opportunity, Dr. Strean, to discuss with you the psychological problems of my colleagues."

She went on, as though speaking confidentially, "Once I was the victim of a very jealous teacher in another school. I suffered so many verbal attacks from her that I had to be hospitalized." She added thoughtfully, "I think persecuting people are attracted to me and want to drive me into hospitals."

"How many times have they driven you into hospitals?" I asked.

"I had to go to hospitals five separate times because people persecuted me so. I was sedated, given shock therapy. I was under so much pressure they even had me talk to psychiatrists. I stayed in one hospital almost six months." She added guiltily, "I have not told the school authorities about my trips to the mental hospitals."

While I had treated some severely emotionally disturbed patients in my office, I never had seen one who had been in and out of five mental hospitals or stayed for as long as half a year. I felt challenged but humbled by the task before me—before both of us, for it would be a task for Nancy too.

Working together we had to uncover the villains in her early life, who she believed had been out to do away with her. I had to help build enough trust between us before she could speak freely of her buried fears, hates and sexual desires.

As I sat listening to Nancy that first session, I asked myself questions that would preoccupy us both for the next several years. What had happened in her childhood that made her judgment, her grasp on reality and her relationships with others so tenuous? What could have caused so much torment that at times she was driven insane?

What had caused her to flee into such dangerous delusions and hallucinations that she could not distinguish fact from fantasy?

Nancy now talked briefly about her husband. "Paul and I were married six years ago. We have a little girl, Sheila, almost four. Paul is an executive at one of New York's largest advertising agencies. He's ten years older than I am. I just celebrated my thirty-sixth birthday. We live in a six-room apartment on Sutton Place."

She lowered her eyes as if ashamed of her marriage. Then she suddenly offered, "I enjoyed him sexually before we married but recently I am turned off. As soon as he comes near I feel nauseated. Sometimes I break out in hives or vomit."

I kept quiet, wanting her to continue. She winced, then said, "Paul is very understanding. He urged me to see you, though the real reason I'm here is because my work is being interfered with. Work is my number-one priority."

Another pause, then: "My husband often seems like two people. Before we married he was warm and appealing. Now he's an agitator, like the principal. Both men want to assault me, to dominate me, to tell me what to do, how to behave. It's as if I have no control."

I thought, And my time will come. She will want to split my personality, believe *I* am the agitator, as she relates to me in the same way she has related to her husband and the principal and to anyone else she believes is threatening her.

I asked, "Tell me something about your parents."

She said, almost a whisper, "My mother died of cancer when I was six years old. I hardly remember her. I think of her as a woman who never said a word but just looked at me sadly. My baby brother Peter was two when she died. I was elected to take care of him when the nurse was not there."

"And your father?"

"He's a prominent gynecologist. He's busy from morning until night, always has been. He never recovered from my mother's death. He refused to marry again though a lot of women pursued him because he's quite handsome. He has intense blue eyes and blond hair. I have my mother's dark hair. Peter has my father's blond hair and blue eyes."

Nancy offered more information about her father at our first session. "He expected me to take over all my mother's work. As I grew up, I had to run the house, supervise the maid and cook, all the while trying to get high marks in school. It was very hard to take care of everybody, especially my brother Peter, who was very high-strung."

She sighed. "I have to admit I felt relieved when Peter went off to prep school at fourteen." She added, "He lives in Los Angeles now. He's a prominent lawyer. We see each other about once a year when one of us travels to the other coast. I have never known whether he was friend or enemy."

There was silence again. I waited for her to go on. She was doing well, considering how frightened she was when she walked into the room forty-five minutes before.

She licked her lips as though they were suddenly dry and said, "My would-be murderers have been so sadistic that many times I really have thought of taking my life."

Then she stared at me as though trying to decide if it was safe to tell me something very secret. Deciding in the affirmative, she went on, "As a matter of fact, I tried to commit suicide several times. Once I took an overdose of sleeping pills. Another time I cut my wrist with a razor and watched the blood spurt out."

I felt myself again becoming anxious, thought, What if Nancy decides to try to commit suicide while working with me? The horror of horrors for any therapist.

I would have to take my chances—that is, if I wanted to try to help this tormented woman who had little respect for or belief in herself. She still blamed herself for her mother's early death, as virtually every child does when a parent dies. She also feared her father's profession as the enemy who had taken him away from her.

I had to show Nancy I understood her pain and at the same time try to relieve it by allowing her to speak of her long-buried fantasies and fears. It was a challenge of the highest order to accept into therapy someone this mentally disturbed, caught in a crosscurrent of the wish to kill and the fear of being killed.

Most psychiatrists and many psychoanalysts do not believe psychotic patients can be helped on the analytic couch. They contend that only drugs or electroshock can ease their suffering. But a few prominent psychiatrists, like Dr. Harold Searles and Dr. Karl Menninger, and psychoanalyst Reuben Fine, have pointed out that patients are far more likely to improve if they find therapists willing to listen to them as they recollect illusions of childhood, along with their intense fears and wishes.

I would be entering dangerous psychic territory but the rewards, if we succeeded, would be high—the recovery of the patient, a recovery that would enable her to lead a more normal life.

I have never been one to resist a challenge. In some aspects I am like my father, the bacteriologist, the researcher. The challenge offered by Nancy stimulated me. Also, she was appealing in manner as she requested me to help her.

I said to her, "Our time is up."

She asked, not daring to look into my eyes, fearing rejection, "Are you going to take me on as a regular patient?"

I responded, "I would like to work with you." I then asked, "Can you come four times a week after your teaching hours?"

She looked relieved, her eyes so grateful I thought she might kiss me. She said, "I could be here by four o'clock."

"Can you make it five? Mondays, Tuesdays, Thursdays and Fridays?"

"Of course," she said.

She stood up and I noticed the blue eyes seemed clearer, less diffused. There was also some deep emotion in them I could not fathom. I hoped someday to see her flash a real smile.

I heard the front door close. I walked over to the window, looked up at the clear sky to the north. I thought, This is a challenge, a powerful challenge, like trying to make par on a long and winding hole where you cannot see the green as you tee off. Sometimes I made par or better but often I was way below par. I wondered, What will this new challenge bring, hoping for a high psychological score.

2
THE
SMOULDERING
RAGE

**Spring
into
Summer
1980**

Nancy arrived for her second appointment showing a certain eagerness not present the first hour. She sat down, without being asked, on the chair she had previously occupied. Then she smiled wanly.

I was silent, waiting for her to speak. She said, "I feel more comfortable today than at our first interview. I somehow feel stronger in coping with my principal."

Then she added in bitter tone, "But he keeps staring at me as if he's plotting my demise."

She seemed at times to speak quite eloquently (particularly when she felt very angry), as befit the poetic soul I learned she was—told me she had written poetry since the age of twelve.

She sat up straight in the chair, looked at me rather grimly. "I feel so victimized I can't concentrate on my work. The principal is threatened by me and furious and envious of my competency. He fuels my colleagues' fire, causing them to act jealous of me, too. They all want me to fail as a teacher."

As I listened, I wondered, And how envious is she of the principal and of his competence? How competitive is she with her colleagues, resenting them in much the same way she resented her father and her brother?

I knew it would be months, maybe years, before Nancy could recognize how much *she* wanted to do battle. Any statement this early on my part about her wish to fight and to conquer others would only be experienced as a slap in the face. I knew the only way I could now respond to Nancy was to listen quietly and nonjudgmentally to her expression of feeling "victimized."

For the first month of her therapy, I listened attentively and said little. She used most of the sessions to talk about the many times she had felt a victim. She started with the present, where she was the victim in her marriage, describing Paul as a "cold, icy, unloving husband." Then she returned to the psychiatrists of her therapeutic past who had "tortured" her with injections and electroshock. Finally, she went back to her childhood, to her father and brother who "always made me feel like a second-class citizen."

Nancy spent her first twelve sessions talking of being "demeaned" and "derogated." I noticed it was largely by men. While she spoke of nurses in mental hospitals as "insensitive" and referred to the "unavailability" of her mother (virtually absent all of Nancy's early life because of cancer), it was principally men who victimized her, she charged.

When she realized I did not comment on her perception of how often she had been mistreated by men, she started to show her first doubts about me.

She remarked in her fifteenth session, "You have been quiet for a long time. I am sure you think very little of me."

She then searched my eyes, as though they would confirm what she believed.

"What gives you this impression?" I asked.

"How can you think well of a woman who has been in a mental hospital on five different occasions and who can't cope with her difficulties in a sane way?" she said slowly.

I kept silent, wanting her to speak on. This she did, in a more hostile tone. "Behind your kind face, Dr. Stream, I am sure you are saying, 'That crazy woman! Who needs her?'"

This meant to me that Nancy bore an intense hate for herself and for men. She could not believe I would possibly accept her, feel empathic and want to help her. I was starting to be perceived by her in the same paranoid way she experienced others, particularly men.

But every analyst knows you can never talk anyone out of a conviction or a perception. Thus I had to take her evaluation of me seriously.

I said, "Since you have been in mental hospitals, what is it about such experiences that I should think less of you for?"

Irritation showed in her eyes, then rage. She countered, "Now you're feigning sincerity. You know goddamned well that anyone who goes to a loony bin is a second-class citizen. I can't see why you should feel different from anybody else in this world who knows that mental hospitals are for crazy people who *are* second-class citizens."

She had projected onto me what she thought of herself. This is how our minds work when we harbor a feeling we cannot tolerate. She really did believe she was a second-class citizen. Given her "history of mental illness," as psychiatrists say, she felt no one could accept her.

I told myself, Look, Strean, this woman needs to criticize you. She has had murder in her heart for a long time and no one has allowed her to talk about it. You must let her tell you what she thinks is wrong with you. I came to this conclusion fairly easily, for at this point in my career I had helped many patients who felt extremely self-critical as a result of emotional conflicts. Also, the years spent in personal analysis accepting my own "craziness" helped me understand the "craziness" in others that appeared in varying degrees.

Thus I had no negative feelings toward Nancy, although earlier in my professional career I would have been thrown by her accusations. I would have felt threatened because, at that time, I believed there was a certain truth in the belief the schizophrenic patient was different from the supposedly sane person. Now I knew Nancy and I were more similar than different, that our differences were a matter of degree. I could accept the "Nancy" in me with a fair amount of equanimity.

What Nancy said was true about many professionals who work with schizophrenic patients. Just as they want to keep their own disturbing thoughts secret from themselves, the presence of a Nancy threatens an awakening of their own irrational, primitive fantasies—fantasies that exist in all of us.

Nancy's paranoia, like a nightmare experienced while awake, corresponded to what most of us sometimes endure whenwe fall asleep and have a bad dream. Anyone who has learned to analyze dreams, which every analyst does, should be accepting of the primitive thoughts of a psychotic. The analyst's dreams and the thoughts of the patient are indeed similar.

Nancy continued to inform me how little I thought of her, and how much I had judged her as incapable of coping with life. I let her express her doubts and criticisms as openly as possible, without a word of censure.

During her second month of treatment I did say, "You feel I'm a punitive judge who isn't here to understand you but to sit in judgment, and who will judge you harshly."

Tears welled in her eyes. She reached for a tissue, blew her nose. Then she said, clutching the tissue, "I've never thought anybody would take the time just to listen to me without thinking evil thoughts about me and toward me."

She fell silent for a moment, then went on: "I'm not sure I can trust you. I've had to deal with evil people all my life. I've only known you less than two months but you have been the first person, as far back as I can remember, who has not criticized me."

More silence, then: "After a month of courtship, Paul, my husband, began to get critical. There's hardly anyone I can think of who sooner or later doesn't strike out at me in a hostile way."

As Nancy said this, I realized that anyone so full of hatred and resentment would have to think chiefly of battle. It would be difficult for her to see me as someone who would refuse to fight with her no matter how hard she tried to provoke the battle.

One of the reasons I believe schizophrenic patients are so difficult to work with is that they are constantly collecting injustices. They find it hard to accept a therapist's benign understanding. The schizophrenic patient puts every therapist to the extreme test. Sooner or later it becomes tempting to wish to fight back when a patient is so full of rage, contempt and lack of appreciation for any offer of help.

I told myself this was just the start of many, many tests Nancy would put me through. Whatever anger or irritation I felt would have to be carefully monitored and analyzed, during and after the sessions.

Although she continued to have her doubts about me, particularly my sincerity, Nancy began to show a small semblance of hope that perhaps I was more interested in helping than hurting her. In her third month of treatment she even said during one session, "When I show irritation toward you or resentment of you, you don't seem to want to retaliate like the other doctors did."

But she did not fully accept this for she then asked, "Isn't that so?"

I showed Nancy she did not truly believe what she had just said. I asked, "You don't quite trust that idea, do you?"

She laughed, then said, "You really understand me, don't you?" Then she complained, "Why can't you reassure me and tell me you're not out to get me? When you don't reassure me, I begin to distrust you, like I distrust everybody else."

The thought of reassuring her, of telling her I was not an evil man but a caring therapist, was tempting. But I knew full well that unless I encouraged all her doubts to emerge, they would remain underground and she would eventually be as paranoid toward me as toward the principal and others in her life.

I made an interpretation. "When you want me to reassure you, you hope to get rid of the discomfort of so many doubts about me."

She looked at me almost in disbelief. Her expression changed from one of serenity to anger. She spit out the words: "You are a pompous ass! You're more interested in making the right interpretations than making me feel comfortable."

She raged on, "You really are an arrogant bastard. You remind me of all those psychiatrists in the mental hospitals. They never reassured me but zapped me with electroshock. Or shoved medicine up my ass. Or drugged me out of my few remaining wits. Now you're shoving your fucking interpretations down my throat."

I felt the full impact in this session of Nancy's acute hatred—a hatred most patients do not feel free to express until far deeper into their analysis. Nancy's blue eyes seemed to project a virulent fury. Her expression mirrored an acute self-hatred as her body shook.

She hurled further accusations. "There's something very

inhumane about you, Strean. You don't want to reassure troubled people. You make them an object of your scientific scrutiny. You really are a cold, heartless bastard."

As I listened to Nancy demean me in a now-sharp, shrill voice, I felt like someone about to be assassinated any moment. My heart beat faster as she called me again and again a vicious, heartless bastard. Overcome with feelings of helplessness, I thought, Can I really help someone with these depths of rage? Am I tackling a degree of emotional illness that is over my head?

Afterward I studied my reactions and thought long and hard about them. I realized Nancy was consumed with hatred, perhaps more than any patient I had ever treated. She wanted to destroy even those who wished to be kind to her. In many ways she found my benign understanding irritating because it thwarted her major way of coping—to fight and fight hard.

As I became aware once again of the helplessness I experienced, I recalled times I felt the victim of someone more powerful, bigger physically as well as intellectually. I realized Nancy was trying to put me in her position—helpless and weak compared to her as oppressor.

My instincts were correct because at the next session she asked, "How do you feel when I let you know what kind of person I think you are?"

I asked, "Do you have any thoughts about how I feel?"

"I think you feel wiped out. Small. And that you hate me for exposing your weakness."

She was telling me how *she* felt when someone opposed or criticized her in any way. I said nothing.

After gloating over exposing my weaknesses, she started

to recall the many times she felt weak and helpless at grammar school and in her Park Avenue home, growing up in the presence of her sharp-witted physician father and equally sharp-witted brother. She compared it to how she felt when she gave birth to a daughter—the weak, helpless female.

As Nancy shared with me her feelings of helplessness, weakness and fragility of ego, she relived a number of upsetting experiences. She spoke of being mocked and derided by her brother, pressured never to show a sign of illness by her father. She also described her deep feelings of desertion as her mother lay dying.

When, for the first time, she talked in great detail of the death of her mother and how abandoned she felt at the age of six, I had to do something that made her feel I was that abandoning mother.

It was now July and I had to inform her my four weeks of summer vacation would start at the end of the month. The summer break is traumatic to most patients for it is felt as desertion. I knew for sure Nancy would not accept it peacefully.

I realized I had taken a gamble when I first started to see her in April, near to vacation, but I sensed she needed my help desperately. I had told her in our second meeting that I would be going on a month's vacation in August even though I knew it did not register because August seemed so far away.

I do not like to begin an analysis in April. It is usually very upsetting for a patient—any patient—to become attached to me and then feel understandably forsaken sixteen weeks later. But I knew if I postponed seeing Nancy until fall, she would feel even more deserted and rejected because of the depths of her "paranoid psychosis."

Every time I, or any analyst, thinks about a patient and what the patient needs, he also has to ask, How deeply and in what way do I want the patient to feel about me? At times I have wanted patients to miss me so I could hold a certain importance in their lives—what my colleagues would call "a need to enhance my own narcissism."

But now I dealt with a woman who believed she lived in real danger, one that might destroy her unless I gave her new strengths in her four weekly visits. Although I wanted Nancy to think of me as helpful, I was deeply concerned about the degree of her emotional illness.

Such state of mind is inherent in those who believe others are out to kill or harm them in devious ways. There is no realistic basis for their fear. Those who suffer from paranoia are convinced they are in dire danger. Nobody loves them, everyone hates them and not a soul wants to help them, they believe.

To this very day, the schizophrenic has been viewed by most people—and by the majority of psychiatrists and other therapists—as "subhuman," crazy, animal-like and terrifying. His speech sometimes does not make sense. He hears voices or he is catatonic, he will not utter one word.

Or he will talk continually about impulses most of us usually repress—sexual and/or violent feelings and wishes. These include committing incest, manifesting acute dependency, wanting to be the opposite gender and what analysts call "polymorphous perverse." The latter applies to cannibalism, as well as smearing feces over one's self or another person, behavior often seen in infants and very young children.

Contrary to conventional popular—and professional—belief, I am convinced the child, man or woman who suffers from schizophrenia in the words of Dr. Harry Stack Sullivan, a pioneer in the treatment of schizophrenic patients, is "more human than otherwise." Such a person is more acutely aware of pain, grief and trauma to the mind than what we call the "average" human being. When the schizophrenic experiences grief, it is likely to be more devastating than the grief of most of us. Neurotics may feel "separation anxiety" when away from someone they love but the schizophrenic experiences holy terror.

The plight of a schizophrenic patient able to function fairly well after he left a mental hospital was portrayed in the 1986 Emmy award—winning Hallmark Hall of Fame television feature, *The Promise.* James Garner played a middle-aged bachelor whose schizophrenic brother, portrayed by James Woods, was released from a mental hospital to live with Garner. For a while the brother acted normally but one day his fantasies overpowered him. Garner's first impulse was to return him to the hospital. Then he realized his brother needed to be with him and that he could cope with his brother's short-term breaks with reality because he loved him, wanted to help him.

The schizophrenic patient needs, I believe, what frightened children require to grow and develop—understanding, tenderness, love and empathy. Humane attitudes on the part of the therapist as he helps the schizophrenic face his conflicts can restore him to a functioning human being able to love and accept love.

Every practitioner of psychoanalytic therapy with schizophrenic patients invariably is asked, "Is there a 'genetic predisposition' toward schizophrenia?" The answer, like most questions, varies with the practitioner. Most of us who conduct psychotherapy with schizophrenics believe the primary roots of schizophrenia lie in the patient's early life with his mother and father. Those who use as "curative" such medical procedures as insulin injections, electroshock, and drugs attribute the cause of schizophrenia to the patient's "genetic endowment."

While everyone is a product of heredity and environment, my own view of schizophrenia is that no one will become schizophrenic if he has experienced an early environment with two parents who love not only him but each other. In my thirty-five years of working with both schizophrenic children and adults, I have never witnessed one case where there was a consistently loving environment in childhood. I have also noticed that when the schizophrenic is provided with a constant warm environment in the form of a competent, caring therapist, he invariably improves.

If schizophrenia were solely a genetic disease, it could not be affected by human encounters alone. While we should never rule out the fact that all of us are born with certain vulnerabilities that affect our emotional adjustment—temperament, energy level and intelligence—it is *how* our parents react to us and *how* we experience their reactions that affect our emotional life more than anything else.

This belief is not the most popular one among mental health professionals who treat schizophrenia. Most professionals see schizophrenia as evolving from hereditary, as well as biological and organic causes. Yet I find it interesting that those who adhere to this viewpoint have never tried doing extensive psychotherapy. Nor have they acknowledged the many methodological flaws in their research that psychoanalytically oriented therapists have consistently exposed.

Very often one way to determine a patient's potential for enhanced maturity is for the analyst to ask himself, How would I feel if I met this person socially? I do this with every patient, male or female. I fantasied meeting Nancy at a bar and knew I would be attracted to her. Her warmth and the feeling that she was genuine came through despite her acute inner distress. At times I fantasied myself as a lover who could be quite tender and erotic toward her. This fantasy gave me hope for her future as a happier wife and mother as a result of the therapeutic process.

At first Nancy did not talk much about her husband and daughter, she was too overwhelmed by her own depression. But slowly she started to describe more of her home life. She and Paul, both busy at work during the week, seldom went out nights, but on Saturdays they often dined at some of the city's leading restaurants, leaving Sheila with her nurse. Occasionally they would ask friends from Paul's advertising agency to their home on a Saturday evening. The cook, Bella, whom Nancy had known since her marriage, prepared the meals. Nancy told me, "I hate to cook. I will not do it."

I asked myself, What about Nancy's strengths? Here was a woman obviously quite paranoid at times, suffering delusions, some of which had been so intense she had to be hospitalized. Yet she could maintain relationships with children at school without appearing emotionally disturbed.

I did not know how apparent to her colleagues and students Nancy's aberrant behavior was at this point in her treatment. But I was reasonably sure they would have to think,

"Something is wrong here." Yet regardless how much of Nancy's conflicts were known by others and regardless of how severely disturbed she was, I was impressed with her abundant energy, her superior intelligence and her creativity. I kept asking myself, Where did she get all these admirable characteristics from?

The answer to this question came from several years of working with schizophrenics. I had originally viewed schizophrenia as a disease that pervades the patient's complete functioning—much like a cancer that consumes one's total being. Then I realized this was a complete misconception.

All of us possess both strengths and limitations, whether we are emotionally mature, neurotic or psychotic. We become unduly anxious in situations we feel dangerous. We may become hypersensitive and suspicious, deeply afraid of certain fantasies. The child, man or woman labeled "schizophrenic" shows both strengths and limitations. His hypersensitivity and suspiciousness are similar to everyone else's, only at times "more so."

Thus, Nancy could be quite paranoid in some areas of her life, show poor judgment about those who angered her while still revealing strengths as a teacher. Just as I had to understand her pathology, I also had to understand her mental health. There were strengths in her life that had helped her become a capable teacher. It was important to take into account these strengths as well as the causes of her hallucinations.

Nancy did not have to work. Her husband earned enough in his advertising agency to support her and their daughter on Sutton Place. But she had become a teacher for many reasons. She had to keep busy intellectually for she could never stay home all day caring for Sheila. Nancy was an achiever, especially when it came to the use of words. As a young girl she started to write poetry and never gave this up. She also tried to give to children what she wanted for herself as a child—a wise, thoughtful, loving teacher.

It was a measure of her mental health that she sought psychoanalysis after so many fruitless, painful experiences in hospitals. This showed a wholesome courage and a certain mature persistency lacking in many who have never been as disturbed as Nancy.

During the first interview, I received one other important clue to Nancy's healthy self as revealed in her teaching. She told me she had chosen me as her analyst because she learned, from my articles and books, how deeply I was concerned with children and how I had helped many to greater happiness during my years of work. She said quietly, "We have a lot in common. I love children too and try to help them in the classroom."

Now Nancy and I were at the start of July, both aware the coming separation would be traumatic for her. In preparation I had said during one session in May, "I'd like to remind you of something I spoke about when we began our work. I will be taking a vacation during the month of August."

Her response was one I learned would be quite characteristic of her—denial. A defense we all use to some degree to avoid facing an event, act or thought that causes us acute anxiety.

Nancy replied in a matter-of-fact tone, as though wishing

me well, "Everybody's entitled to a vacation." She added, "As a teacher, I get a vacation from teaching. You get yours from analyzing."

I said to myself, The lady sounds too accommodating, she is engaging in what analysts call the defense of "reaction formation." Nancy was saying the exact opposite of what she felt so she could protect against feelings of hate toward me. Instead of telling me what a son of a bitch she felt I was for leaving her to go on vacation, she told me I deserved one.

It was clear to me that Nancy felt emotionally abandoned by her mother's early death. She also had been deserted emotionally by her father, brother, husband, previous therapists, friends and colleagues. Analysts know that what happens in the analytic room recapitulates and mirrors what has happened in the life of the patient. Nancy was doomed to feel abandoned, deserted and rejected by me as she thought of my leaving her for a month.

The sensitive therapist knows that when a patient protects himself by the defense of reaction formation, you have to respect the fact that he is too afraid to speak the truth. From the start of therapy to its finish, each patient defends himself in his own unique, characteristic fashion. What have been defenses in daily living become resistance in therapy. If someone rationalizes, denies or projects difficulties onto others in daily life, this is what he will do in therapy.

When the patient feels very disturbed, as Nancy did at the start of treatment, the therapist must respect the resistance. Otherwise, the patient will feel attacked and become even more acutely disturbed, withdrawing to an even more remote extent.

As I have told students over the years, defenses are like skin. They protect the human being from painful stimuli, both internal and external. If you pierce skin too deeply, blood flows. The psychological "skin" of patients must be protected, especially the "thin skin" of the psychotic patient, who reacts with intense emotion to anything he believes is an attack.

Therefore I did not push Nancy to discuss her feelings about the summer break. But as is true with virtually every patient in analysis, denial never works completely. What is being protected shows itself in disguised form sooner or later.

Though Nancy did not talk directly about my going away, she did speak of the summer when she was five years old and her mother and father flew to Europe, leaving her and her brother with a baby-sitter.

Nancy said, referring to her parents, a stricken look in her luminous eyes, "How could they do this to me? How could they leave me with a stranger I hardly knew, and a baby brother who was nothing but a burden?"

Tears rolled down her cheeks as she reached for a tissue from the box on the table in front of her, wiped her eyes. Without verbalizing it, I was pleased she was feeling freer to show me her emotions. The more we offer our hidden feelings to the light of reason, the mentally healthier we feel.

Nancy spent several sessions talking about how "cruel" her mother and father had been and how unfeeling the baby-sitter, whom she described as a two-hundred-pound, red-faced Irish woman, seemed.

"She ate everything in the house and sometimes even snatched food from my plate," Nancy said indignantly.

It was clear to me that I was being experienced unconsciously by Nancy as both her abandoning parents and the hungry baby-sitter. By early July, it was still premature to face Nancy with how angry she felt at me for daring to leave her. She wasn't yet ready to confront her thoughts of me as that unfeeling, selfish "baby-sitter."

During the second week of July, she related one of the first dreams in her treatment. "I was yelling and screaming at my Aunt Helen. Instead of hugging and kissing me, she ignored me," Nancy said. Then she stopped and looked at me with a sad expression on her face.

I asked, "Tell me your thoughts about the dream." Through what analysts call "free association," we could reach the deeper meaning of the dream and decode it.

"I thought I could trust my Aunt Helen but she was the kind of woman who, every time I thought she loved me, would sooner or later turn her back on me," Nancy said.

She added, "Aunt Helen died last year and I didn't know whether to cry or feel happy she no longer would suffer pain from the cancer in her lungs. She had smoked heavily since she was sixteen."

As Nancy talked on about her aunt, I learned her last name was Smith, therefore she had my initials, "H. S." I have discovered that when patients dream of people in their past or present, they are often dreaming about the analyst. One clue is that the name's initials are the same. I remembered a patient, treated years before, who constantly suffered nightmares in which Dr. Harry Stack Sullivan appeared and yelled and screamed at him. Dr. Sullivan and I also have the same initials, "H. S. S."

I asked Nancy, "Why do you think you were dreaming about your Aunt Helen last night?"

"Well, we've been talking about my parents disappointing me during the month of August when they went to Europe. And Aunt Helen would also go to Europe during the summer months and never even send me a postcard."

"Do you think I'm going to Europe this summer?"

"It's funny that you ask." She gave a nervous laugh. "I was discussing vacations today with a fellow teacher who is also in analysis and we both agreed that all analysts seem to to travel to Europe in August, so you must be going too."

I could now offer Nancy my first major interpretation. I said, "You really feel I am like your Aunt Helen and you don't know if you can depend on me. Sometimes you feel I am warm and caring but other times you feel I don't give a damn about you. As we get ready for my vacation, it is hard for you to tell me how hurt and angry you feel toward me. Just as it was difficult to tell your parents and Aunt Helen you felt lonely and deserted."

Nancy did not say a word. She just stared at me. But it was quite clear she heard me as suddenly this soft-spoken woman turned into a violent attacker.

She literally bellowed. It was the *second* time she had raised her voice in the office. "You remind me of Dr. Levy, who treated me for six months and then said I was too sick to be treated analytically. He insisted I needed drugs and electroshock. He had a good reputation but he really was a miserable bastard. He was scared to work with somebody like me."

I was not surprised by her change of mood. I expect this instability, particularly from severely emotionally damaged patients. It is difficult for them to control their feelings for long if they feel attacked.

I asked Nancy, "What do you think Dr. Levy was scared of that made him stop working with you so abruptly?"

"He was scared of my anger," she said, her voice returning to normal. "And scared of my neediness. He put me in a mental hospital when I told him I wanted to see him more often. He said I needed constant care."

I thought to myself, the schizophrenic has been so deprived emotionally as a child that he *is* insatiable when it comes to the care he needs.

I said, "Right now it is hard for you to tell me how much I seem like Dr. Levy. You feel I am giving up on you at a time you want more of me. And you are very angry at me."

She stared at me once again. Then, rather abruptly, she clammed up for the rest of the session, which had about ten minutes left. Several sessions later, however, she was able to speak a vital truth, a truth so buried all her life that it had helped bring on her madness.

She said, "You're pressuring me to tell you how I feel about your going on vacation. I know that. This pressure you're putting on me feels like shock therapy. You bang away at me like Dr. Levy arranged for them to do in the hospital. It's like you're hitting my head against a stone wall."

She waited for me to speak, I kept silent.

She went on, anger again in her voice, "If you really cared about me, or if any of the stupid shrinks who saw me cared about me, you wouldn't go on a long vacation to Europe.

You're sending me in effect to Siberia, because you hate me. You're no different from Aunt Helen or my parents and all the unfeeling, hostile bastards I've had to live with my whole life—including my husband."

At times Nancy sounded like a truck driver. The wish to use vulgar language lies in all of us. It is the child's way of rebelling against what he believes cruel parental regulations. Many of my patients use words not in parlor language. If the analyst shows disgust or disapproval, the patient may be afraid to express himself, feel chastised. He must be allowed to speak freely of his inner demons in any way he chooses, whether with vulgarity or in the best of taste.

Her rage was intense and I could feel my heart beat faster as she expressed it. I also knew this was one of the few times in her life that a parental figure had tried to help her say what she really thought and felt. I wanted to understand her acute rage, instead of threatening to punish her, encourage her to speak of it, face it, so it would no longer poison her emotionally.

Hers was the rage of a child unable to cope with overwhelming feelings of abandonment and hate, an abandonment that felt like annihilation. Many children retreat into autism, losing even their ability to speak, because their feelings of being deserted threaten to overwhelm them. Every child feels this rage to a certain degree when parents leave him for a short time and he finds himself in the care of strangers. But the child who becomes a schizophrenic adult hides very severe traumas from early years. These traumas must emerge and be confronted in therapy for him to feel at peace.

I could not guess this early in therapy the nature of

Nancy's traumas. She would have to give me clues through her words. This would take time—months, perhaps years. It was a commitment that most therapists in overcrowded mental hospitals, as well as many of those in private practice, were not willing to give.

I assured her, "It's very helpful to our work for you to tell me exactly what you feel, particularly about being abandoned."

She burst suddenly into tears, then said brokenly, "I feel like a helpless baby, like I'm in a playpen crying for my mother and there's nobody to comfort me."

Nancy's pain was intense. She was living not in fantasy but in cruel reality.

She mopped at her eyes, went on, "Much of my childhood was spent alone, feeling furious and unloved. I wanted so much to be held tenderly and taken care of—not raped emotionally."

I heard the word "rape," filed it away for future reference. Nancy exaggerated, as many patients do, but being "raped" had some important meaning to her that, I thought, I would discover eventually.

When that session ended I felt we had made much progress. It was only the beginning, but it was a first step in the battle to gain Nancy's release from the destructive fantasies that held her in their vicelike grip.

Throughout the month of July, Nancy vacillated between expressing her anger, feeling like a helpless baby convinced she was going to die, and trying to manipulate me to stay in New York and continue to see her.

She begged during one session in mid-July, "What can

I do to get you to give up your vacation and help me? I am falling apart. Have you no heart?"

Then she threatened, "If you don't stay I am sure I will either kill myself, hunt you down and kill you, or go into a mental hospital."

This was not the first time a patient had so threatened me but Nancy seemed to have more conviction about killing herself or me than any previous patient. Not only had she been hospitalized on five occasions but had tried suicide four times, I had learned. Twice she had slashed her wrists, another time she swallowed an entire bottle of aspirin and was in a coma for two weeks. In the fourth attempt she'd tried to starve herself.

The patient's history of hospitalizations and suicide attempts is very important to the analyst. Nancy's attempted suicides gave me every reason to believe she might try to kill herself or me and then become hospitalized once more.

I felt a variety of intense emotions this July 1980. I asked myself on more than one occasion, Why the hell did you take this case on? You will only worry throughout your vacation about Nancy killing herself or tracking you down and trying to kill you. I recall saying to myself, In so many ways she seems like a manipulative bitch. Goddamn her, she wants me to suffer if I do not become an all-giving, always-present mother. I started to feel sorry for myself.

While I had felt emotionally impotent before, this was one of the angriest moments of my life as an analyst, and I had been a psychoanalyst for over twenty years.

As I analyzed my own feelings—part of the daily work

of the analyst—I realized some of my anger was caused by her puncturing my narcissism and omnipotence as an analyst. In addition, my feelings of helplessness and anger now mirrored Nancy's. She *wanted* me to feel as she felt—raging and helpless. Then she would not be so alone. We would be like siblings under the skin. In her fantasy, I represented not only her lost mother but her father and brother as well.

As I became more aware of my reactions to her vitriolic displays, I finally could tell her, just before we parted, "I think you would like me to feel as upset about my going away as you are."

She looked at me, a hint of a twinkle in those blue eyes, said, "You're actually right. You're getting away with murder. I want you to realize you are not compassionate and should suffer as much as I do."

The more Nancy could discharge her hatred and reveal the abandoned little girl within who yearned for love and care, the more she would be able to cope with her day-to-day life. My task was to help her achieve this understanding.

In the last session, the day before I left for my vacation (not in Europe but in the Adirondacks), Nancy admitted, "I think I can manage on my own but I am not sure. I am going to write you a letter or two during August, whether or not you approve."

Without protesting or approving her pronouncement, I told her, "I'll see you the day after Labor Day in September."

As she walked out the door, she had a sad look on her face. She waved as though trying to reassure me she would be all right.

3
THE
SOUND
OF ANGER

Fall
1980

I enjoyed my summer vacation in the Adirondacks as I swam, played golf and contemplated the majestic beauty of the mountains. It was a relaxing respite from the taxing duties of life in Manhattan.

Like all analysts, I work very hard almost all year. Most people, including patients, do not realize what it is like to sit hour after hour quietly listening to the psychic traumas of men and women. Your feet become paralyzed, you feel thirsty and hungry. If you move a muscle the patient complains that you are not listening. Even if you have a cold or an acute physical pain, you must show up for the sessions or your patients will feel even more depressed. Sometimes you work ten to twelve hours a day, every day of the week except Sunday. And even then patients phone and ask for an appointment, saying they are suffering a crisis.

At odd moments on vacation I felt Nancy might actually try suicide, as she threatened. Or, feeling a bit paranoid, I wondered if she would somehow track me down, force me back to the city with pleas she was near death—or even try to kill me for deserting her.

As I reviewed some of our work over the past four months, I realized Nancy had not spent much time describing her day-to-day life, except for the first month when she talked of her principal and colleagues. At times I wondered if her husband and daughter Sheila were still part of her life, since their absence in her sessions was quite conspicuous.

I realized that Nancy was herself like a little girl who found in me a combination of mommy, daddy and baby-sitter. To talk of her husband or daughter would have made her more of an adult than she cared to be.

During August I received two letters from her, addressed to my office, then forwarded to the Adirondacks. She wrote in the first: "I am having a dismal, depressing summer while you have a wonderful time. I think you are cruel to abandon me and I am not sure I will be working with you in the fall. You are also sadistic, narcissistic and stupid. I think you are in this business for yourself just as your lousy vacation is for yourself, without a thought for your patients. You are a deep disappointment to me. I feel like signing this letter 'Fuck you.' "

Later in the month a second letter arrived, which showed she had turned her hatred on herself. It held no salutation, merely stated: "I continue to be miserable and have thought of ending my life several times. I feel abandoned and worthless and exceedingly despondent. If it were not for Sheila and my students, I would be dead now. I might be before you return. It's hard to say."

I felt reassured by this letter. At least Nancy was alive and protesting. But this feeling did not last long after my return to the city.

Nancy walked belligerently into my office the afternoon following Labor Day. Her eyes flashed as she announced, "I want to show you where and how I tried to kill myself. Look at the scar my knife left."

She started to raise her pale green silk blouse to reveal her stomach. Nancy was my first and only patient that day. I had scheduled all others for the following day knowing that Nancy would appreciate a session the moment I returned. Now I thought, What a hell of a way to begin a new analytic year. Here's this woman lifting her blouse to show me a self-inflicted wound that she blames on me.

Trusting my intuition, I told myself, She wants to get undressed not only to reveal the wound she felt I caused but also to stimulate me sexually. She must feel excited to see me but also furious at being deserted. Hence, all this agitation.

These thoughts consumed about six seconds, then I quickly told her, "It would be best if you sit down and talk to me about your wound rather than show me the scar."

Standing even straighter, she insisted, "It's a big cut and I have to show you so you will understand the depths of my despair this summer." She started again to lift her blouse.

"Please sit down." My voice was the nearest I had ever come to an order with any patient.

She let go of her blouse. Then she made a surprising move. She walked toward me, tried to hug me. I could empathize with the loneliness and desperation she felt—it was that of a forsaken, helpless child who craves protection from a parent. Part of me wanted to hug her just to reassure her she was safe but I knew this would only stimulate her to want physical contact. The analyst has to guard against any such contact with a patient for the latter will only wish more and more. And as most patients usually perceive the analyst as a parental figure, touching or kissing are inevitably experienced as sexual seduction by an exploitative parent—which in turn prompts incestuous desires and fantasies.

As I reflected on Nancy's self-inflicted wound and other physical complaints, they seemed to me the manifestation, albeit imagined, of emotional scars occasioned by my vacation. The need to slash herself had been a replay in many ways of how she felt when her mother died.

It never helps patients to allow them to act out their impulses, as Nancy was trying to do. If the therapist permits this, he becomes the indulgent parent, thwarting one of the major goals of psychoanalysis—to help the patient understand and master wishes rather than impulsively act them out.

I was quite sure Nancy knew this. She had to have heard it from some of the psychiatrists who tried to help her. Nonetheless, she was so furious at me, so agitated by my leaving her for a month, that by being provocative, she hoped to provoke me into an intense fight and thus release her pent-up rage.

She experienced my attempt to curb her acting-out as a further frustration. She said, with passionate fury, "You have no mercy! You have no compassion! All you care about is yourself. You are a narcissistic bastard. You don't want to look at the wounds you inflicted. You only want to talk and get away with murder."

Once again Nancy tried to show me her wound and once again I said, "It will be much more helpful for you to talk rather than to act."

She nearly spit at me as she said, "You remind me of the lousy principal at school, whose hatred brought me here. You're also just like those corrupt doctors who abandoned me in the hospitals. And you're like my mother and father. You don't give a damn, do you?"

She went on, refusing to sit down, "Just as I decided I am never going to have anything to do with all of them, I am not going to have anything to do with you. You don't even want to look at my wound. You just want to *talk* about it in a didactic way. You *are* a son of a bitch!"

She flung me a look of abject hatred and then collapsed into the chair.

I slowly sat down in mine, remained silent. Nancy resumed her harangue. "These past four weeks have been sheer terror, Strean. You're a big tease, I've decided. You seemed to care when you first met me, but obviously you don't give one damn, otherwise you could not have left me alone. You're just like my husband. When I met Paul, he was warm and tender, but after the honeymoon he withdrew. There are two Pauls and there are two Streans."

I still said nothing and she went on, "I could tell over the summer Paul didn't give a damn about me and didn't offer once to take care of Sheila. Just like you don't care about me." She paused, as though delivering a bombshell, "Just as you decided to leave me, I have decided to leave you."

She then retreated into silence, would not speak for half an hour. She sat stolidly in her chair, a look of defiance on her sensitive face. I decided to wait it out and we both sat in silence.

Ten minutes before the end of her hour, I said, "I know how furious and upset you feel at my taking a vacation, but I want to talk to you about your wish to leave therapy before you act on it."

To my surprise, she said, in almost a little-girl voice, "Oh, you don't want to throw me out? You want me to stay? In spite of all those terrible things I said about you?"

Then she laughed, like a child delighted that her mother and father had shown some sign of love and affection.

Although Nancy was relieved this September that I did not intend to desert her, she still showed deep distrust. In the second week after the summer break, she again wanted me to inspect her self-inflicted injury. When I still refused, she broke into another tirade.

"You goddamned bastard!" she charged. "I want my body soothed because I feel deep pain. If you'll understand my pain, I'll know you really care. But your stupid psychoanalytic bullshit makes you just like my father, a cold bastard."

She stared at me as if ready to be rebuked, like a child who had just attacked a parent. I wondered if somewhere along the way her father, the gynecologist, had hurt her physically when he attended to her bodily pains. I would bet that as a child, she heard him use the same language she was now using about me. But I did not say a word, except perhaps through my facial expression, which, I hoped, encouraged her to tell me more.

Nancy then recalled times in her life when she either felt abandoned or was, in fact, abandoned. She said, in a far calmer tone, "I was sent to nursery school when I was three without any warning. Chucked right out of my home. My mother was sick and one day my father took me to this strange place and dumped me with grown-ups and children I didn't know."

She went on, "Then when I was five, I was dispatched to a summer camp by a lake without any explanation. Again I felt cast out.

"When my mother died, I felt I was alone in the middle of the Sahara Desert. I was sure I would perish of starvation."

I commented, "I can understand why you are so angry at me. You believe that, like your mother and father, I've abandoned you, left you alone in the desert to starve."

With a new expression on her face, one of half-trust, Nancy asked in a choked voice, "Since you seem to understand me so well and know what I feel, how could you possibly go on vacation and leave me alone?"

Her voice, I noted, sounded soft, melodious, devoid of rage, as it had in her first session. It was as if, in spite of her hurt, Nancy forgave me for abandoning her.

During the following sessions Nancy spoke more rationally, even though she compared me once again to her hostile principal, her previous, hated therapists and her despised parents. "Like you, they all started off being nice but ended up bastards," she accused.

Then, in a fairly calm voice: "You're like my father, who superficially cared but was very selfish. And my mother, who lived in her own world and couldn't take care of me or show any love."

She fell silent, then added, "Over the summer, a couple of times I felt you had died and were never coming back."

"Like your mother, who died when you were six and never came back?" I asked.

She said, again in angry tone, "I hated my mother for dying. Just like I hated you for abandoning me this summer."

I pointed out, "You are so frightened of your angry feelings toward me, particularly your fantasies of wanting to kill me, that you injured yourself instead of hurting me."

I thought of how often patients who are suicidal, self-hating, deprived of love as children, prefer to destroy themselves physically or psychologically rather than face their rage and murderous feelings toward the important people in their lives—parents, employers or therapists. It is necessary to help every patient feel secure when expressing rage toward the therapist, rather than taking it out on himself. This was particularly vital for Nancy. She rarely had the chance during childhood to air her angry, terrorizing feelings.

Just as the patient wonders, Will the analyst understand me, be empathic and emotionally accept me?, many laymen find it hard to realize the analyst also faces these questions: Will the patient accept me and want to work with me? Will the patient listen to my interpretations and find them helpful?, or will he reject them, time after time, then leave treatment.

These doubts, which face every analyst and patient at the start of treatment, were intensified both for Nancy Winthrop and me. Though she was not completely aware of her feelings, she possessed profound doubts about my capabilities. More than half a dozen psychiatrists and other professionals had failed to help her. She showed deep hatred and distrust of them. Why should I be different?

For a few months in the fall of 1980, she could not quite believe I wanted to understand her threats of suicide and homicide, rather than censure her. She seemed at times perplexed because I wished to help her face and master her intense hatred rather than punish her for feeling and verbalizing it.

Nancy had to doubt my intentions because her entire life she had been disappointed by and suspicious of men. Her gynecologist father, her lawyer brother, her advertising agency husband, were all men to whom she could show only limited love. She hid her intense animosity.

My doubts about successfully treating Nancy were stronger than with other patients. In many ways, I was challenging the establishment. Most psychoanalysts, starting with Freud, held deep doubts as to whether psychoanalysis can be used as the treatment of choice for the schizophrenic patient. According to Freud, the patient, because of his unbridled narcissism, cannot truly relate to another human being because he is too preoccupied with his own emotional neediness and conflicts. He acts like an infant much of the time, completely unaware of the needs of anyone else. He views everyone as existing only to gratify his wishes and demands.

To this day, many psychiatrists and psychoanalysts believe the schizophrenic patient is so fragile emotionally that he cannot look at his life, his dreams, his fantasies, with any degree of detachment and awareness or with what we call the "observing ego." Instead, he must use all his energy to protect himself from feeling rejected, hated, annihilated.

Frequently, one of his deepest fears is that enemies are out to kill him. This was apparent with Nancy in the first interview, when she spoke of her principal and her colleagues wanting to murder her.

In psychoanalysis the couch is usually used for the patient to lie on, as he regresses in his thoughts, says whatever comes to mind. Different analysts begin using the couch at different times. Some request the patient at once to lie down, others wait until the patient makes the suggestion.

I am one who waits until I feel the patient and I have started what is called in "psychoanalese" the "therapeutic alliance," in other words, a working relationship. Many analysts have suggested that a schizophrenic patient is incapable of forming a therapeutic alliance. I disagreed with this notion, but had wanted first to find out who Nancy was, as an analysand. Therefore, we had face-to-face sessions four times a week for many months.

That December Nancy admitted, for the first time, "I am beginning to see you're different from those psychiatrists who gave me shock or drugged me if I showed any hate. And you're different from my parents, who never wanted to hear me out when I felt frightened or abandoned."

I suddenly became aware that, as Nancy felt more accepted and understood, her paranoia began to diminish. She now was less suspicious of the principal, more cordial toward her husband, more patient with her daughter, Sheila. This often happens in therapy—when the child in the adult feels more understood and accepted, the patient more easily tolerates his own children and the child in other adults.

After eight months of treatment, Nancy was clearly in what my analyst, Reuben Fine, describes as the "honeymoon phase." This lasts between three months and a year, as the patient is given the opportunity to say whatever comes to mind without being censored or questioned by the analyst. The patient begins to like himself more and falls in love with the analyst who has provided such a pleasurable environment, one in which the patient feels fully accepted. This is a unique experience. It rarely happens in life and, if it happens at all, occurs in the first few months of infancy or in the first stages of falling "in love."

While Nancy was in the honeymoon phase, I felt pleased

with her progress. I began once again to question Freud's contention that the schizophrenic patient's self-absorption prevents him from forming a therapeutic alliance with the analyst. But Nancy, who had certainly displayed a great deal of hatred, distrust and narcissism, after eight months of analysis could recognize she had received a "different response" from me than from all her other previous "caretakers."

To be able to make this differentiation, she proved that with all the misery she had endured, she still possessed some ability to test reality, to discriminate between those who cared and those who did not. I have often thought one of the reasons Freud and other analysts have been so pessimistic about the treatment of the very disturbed patient is that in Freud's day, analysis was short—a year at the most, frequently only seven months. Nancy took eight months merely to begin to trust me. This is something other therapists who have given up working with schizophrenic patients have not considered enough, I believe.

I was feeling, at this point in her treatment, like the foster parent with a very disturbed child. Often a benign and caring foster parent becomes the recipient of intense hatred from such a child. Many foster parents cannot understand why, since they feel loving, kind and helpful.

It took me many years to realize that the disturbed child, or the very disturbed adult, like Nancy, easily acts venomously toward me because he feels I can take it. As I listened to Nancy, I did not condemn or advise, so she could be more herself, without worrying whether I would hate her.

Because she was starting to reveal the "observing ego," which heralded the beginning of trust in me and the analytic process, I suggested one day, "It would help our work if you used the couch."

Although she now felt more friendly toward me, this new suggestion aroused Nancy's doubts and suspicions. She sat defiantly in her chair, turned quite paranoid as she stated in a loud, angry voice, "You don't want to look at me, do you?"

I kept silent. She went on angrily, "You want to nap, don't you, when you feel tired of me. You don't want any face-to-face contact. You're trying to get rid of me."

She took a deep breath, went on, "As a matter of fact, you're just like Freud. He explained he used the couch because he couldn't stand people looking at him all day."

I was accustomed to patients quoting and misquoting Freud. Though this one was accurate, it did not fully explain why he sat behind the patient. Freud wished to provide a more relaxing atmosphere for the patient, as well as himself, so patient and analyst could devote full attention to the patient's words. This arrangement enabled both participants to examine the patient's fantasies, dreams and memories as well as feelings towards the analyst.

I sat in silence as Nancy's rage escalated. She again charged, "You are probably the most narcissistic man I have ever met."

I thought, She was probably called "narcissistic" by her psychiatrists, since that was Freud's word to describe why the schizophrenic patient could not be helped. In essence, a psychiatrist would be telling her he could not help her in a way that would only intensify her agony and anger.

Nancy spit out the words, "You are not here to help me! You want to help yourself. Sometimes I think you're more selfish than my father and brother. And often I think that like Jerry, my principal, *you're* out to get me."

Silence. Her next thoughts, "You want me to lie down and be your slave, don't you? Well, I'm not ready for that."

I was not going to push her to accept the couch. For the next few sessions she continued to berate me, sat defiantly in the chair, angrily denounced me for daring to suggest she lie on the couch. She accused me of being a "charlatan" as well as a "narcissist." I was a combination of her selfish husband, her principal, her father and brother—all the men she hated.

Just as earlier she had been surprised when I patiently listened to her angry outbursts and did not retaliate, Nancy was equally surprised when I tried empathically to understand her dread of the couch. At one point during her angry refusals to lie down, she asked fearfully, "Are you going to *insist* I take to the couch?"

I sensed how fearful she was, almost in shock at the thought of lying down, feeling exposed in mind and body. I replied, "The analyst never insists. He only tries to understand. I am more interested in understanding your dread of the couch than forcing you to lie down."

Nancy clearly viewed the couch with terror, as though it portended some sexual assault. I thought, She sees me in some way as her physician father who, as she experienced and fantasied him, manipulated her for his own selfish purposes rather than tried to help her gain a sense of self-esteem.

Nancy was not conscious of this connection at such an early stage in treatment but I hoped she would be able to see it as I slowly appeared to her as very different from her dominating father. I learned, over and over, that when I listened rather than talked, tried to understand rather than manipulate, Nancy saw me more realistically as helper rather than exploiter.

After a month of angrily denouncing me and the couch and once again questioning the value of therapy, she told me, "I have just read a textbook on psychoanalysis in which the author points out that the couch fosters expression of memories, fantasies and dreams and can help an analysis."

Then, for the first time in months, she suddenly smiled. There followed a chuckle and the question, "Should I believe that?"

I suggested, "Part of you would like to believe it but you can't quite trust the idea."

"Sometimes I feel you understand me perfectly," she admitted. "You're right. I'd like to try the couch but I'm afraid it might not work. I was never on a couch in my previous therapy and I don't know what to do. I'm frightened."

I felt a little like a hopeful lover, as though my partner acted warm and sexual but refused to undress and lie down on the bed. I wondered if Nancy felt some desire to tease me but could not be sure whether this feeling came from her or me or both of us.

When I was a young analyst I might have been tempted to blurt out to Nancy or a similar patient, "You're trying to tease me." But the analyst must never accuse a patient—this only repeats and enforces childhood trauma.

With experience I had learned to monitor my feelings more wisely. I was convinced the analyst-as-scientist must get significant data from the patient before he declares something conclusive. So I now continued to wait it out, feeling like a frustrated lover.

Slowly Nancy became aware of what analysts call "countertransference" (my feelings toward her). She said one morning, "You're eager for me to take to the couch and disappointed I haven't done so. But I have to test you to see if what you said a couple of months ago is true. Are you really interested in understanding and helping me?"

Her words told me many things. Nancy was perceiving me realistically, something I have noticed that the more disturbed person can often do better than the less disturbed one. Needing as a child to diligently monitor her difficult parents, she became hypersensitive to them. She was now hypersensitive to the analyst's every move—in a way she had become an extremely sensitive psychologist.

Many other patients would not have sensed what I felt at this time, probably because they trusted me more than Nancy did. Though she now felt more positive toward me, this placed her in a quandary. Part of her wished to please me and lie on the couch, part of her still distrusted me.

I felt it crucial for her emotional development to give her as much time as she needed in the chair. As she sensed this, she slowly changed her mind.

One day in late December she said suddenly in a soft voice, her eyes looking squarely into mine, "I'd like to try the couch. But if it doesn't work, I'll race back to the chair."

Then she asked, politely, "Is that acceptable to you?"

I had to be careful, remain the neutral analyst. I replied, "You feel less frightened of the couch but still have your doubts."

I did not want to tell her what to do. I wanted her to make up her own mind, take a step toward that goal of goals—maturity.

Rather than discuss the matter further, she stood up and walked over to the couch, like a soldier advancing cautiously into enemy territory. It was late in her hour, which started at five in the afternoon, following her daily classes.

Most patients are tentative and anxious as they first lie down on the analytic couch. Nancy's sudden change shocked me somewhat. Was she enacting a dream, telling truthfully how she felt, or perhaps combining both? I wondered.

She lay down gingerly, stretched out her slim legs, sheathed in black silk stockings, her feet in black patent-leather pumps with two-inch heels as always. She seemed a different person—that session and the following ones. I hardly recognized her as the woman on the chair who had faced me those early months.

As I saw Nancy lying on the couch in such a seductive posture, I had several fantasies, including joining her there. I had learned by this time in my professional career that such fantasies, if faced and understood, are not to be condemned but serve as a sign of emotional involvement with the patient, not only as a therapist but as a man with a woman.

As I pointed out in *Behind the Couch: Revelations of a Psychoanalyst*, those therapists who cannot tolerate or acknowledge their own sexual fantasies toward an attractive woman lying on a couch are frightened not only of their own impulses but frightened too of the patient. Such therapists make themselves curious automatons, and eventually may incur ulcers or a heart attack as they repress their sexual and other fantasies.

Nancy now spoke in a low but audible tone. "You have seduced me, I feel really turned on. I would love you to lie down next to me, put your arms around me. It's taken a long time to tell you this, but I think you're the most handsome man in the world, the kindest man in the universe. And," she paused, then went on unabashedly, "the sexiest stud in America."

She spoke of me as a prurient sexual object and I knew, in part, she was experiencing me as her seductive and idealized father, who had been in childhood her doctor, as I now was. Perhaps after her mother's death he had at times taken her into his bed to "lie down" next to him, for his comfort and hers. But it would not have been to her therapeutic advantage for me to point this out so early in her analysis. She needed to express without impunity, without censure, all her sexual fantasies and then we would slowly analyze them. Had I said a word, I would have blocked the flow of her thoughts, interfered with her unconscious journey into the traumatic past.

Sexual fantasies by themselves do not tell us much. For one patient, the wish to be hugged can represent a desire to be a baby in his mother's arms. For another, it may mean foreplay in a more adult way. It is crucial for the analyst to understand the fantasies that propel the sexual wishes. Since Nancy showed serious sexual problems in her marriage, it was important to learn what earlier fantasies made her anxious and guilty, interfered with her adult sexual desires and pleasures.

It did not take long to understand that her sexual "trans-ference" was that of a infant wanting to merge with a loving mother and father. Every patient, every human being, has strong wishes to remain an infant and fully loved all the time by a caring mother and father. No one of us is exempt from this wish. We go to our graves possessing it.

As a matter of fact some contemplate death with a certain amount of pleasure. They fantasy being immersed in "mother" earth—rejoining the mother, so to speak.

Nancy's wish to merge with a loving mother and father in an embrace that would last forever was stronger than that of most patients. Neglected from birth by an ill mother, com-pletely abandoned when her mother died, tantalized by her physician father's stimulating but cold ministrations when she was ill, Nancy yearned for me to be the loving mother and father she never had.

This is what analysts mean by "transference." The pa-tient transfers onto the analyst all he wished from his parents and others close to him. But he also transfers what he fears his parents and others would do if he dared show directly what he wanted. This is why analysis takes such a long time. The patient wants to be the most adored infant in the world but fears the analyst will censure him for his forbidden wishes, sexual and violent, from masturbation to murder.

Furthermore, if the patient was actually deprived of loving physical contact as a child, as Nancy was, the wish to be very close physically to the analyst would be strong, as well as terrifying. This is how Nancy felt as she expressed her early sexual desires.

As she yearned to be close to me sexually, she felt on

the one hand like a very excited little girl, but on the other, like a very fearful little girl. She told me that session of dreams and fantasies, of hugging me passionately. She said, "That's why I wanted you to lie down next to me, even though I was afraid you'd think me a pest."

A few days later, feeling somewhat more at ease on the couch, she confessed, "I'd love to live with you, be with you day and night."

Then she added in a tone of self-hatred, "I'm really a leper."

The image of being a leper is not uncommon in the minds of very disturbed patients like Nancy. They demand many things from the analyst—including total love—then feel what they seek is so forbidden they believe they deserve the punishment of leprosy—an illness that ends in sudden death and for which there is no cure.

My task with Nancy, as I viewed it at this point in treatment, was to help her accept with more equanimity her infantile wishes. If she could feel I accepted her in spite of her forbidden fantasies, her self-esteem would rise. She would not seem to herself so "leprous."

This is what all analysts try to do—become more of a benign "super-ego," to be more accepting of the patient's infantile wishes than the parents or the patient ever were. When Nancy told me she wanted to be with me all the time, hold me close forever, but this made her feel like a leper, I pointed out, "You are your own severest critic. You hate yourself for your very human wishes."

At first she responded with relief and pleasure, then feeling guilty again, she remarked sadly, "What you say feels good, if only it were true. But you're feeding me the analysts' party line. How could you possibly love a leper, or a clinging infant? How could you feel anything but contempt for me?"

Abruptly she added, "I don't trust you!"

I thought she genuinely meant every word she uttered, but she was also looking for reassurance. She was saying, Convince me that what you're telling me is true even though I do not believe it.

No patient can be convinced of anything quickly. It takes many, many months, often years, of going over the same fears, memories, wishes and feelings before a patient can change his distorted self-image. He has long repressed his destructive feelings to protect his conscious self from shame, humiliation and psychic pain.

I told Nancy, "You'd like to believe me when I say you are your severest critic but you don't trust me. You feel I'm intolerant. You felt as a child that your parents were intolerant of you and now you believe I feel the same way."

She started to recall memories. "At two years I was crying out, 'I want my mother.' I always yearned for someone to hold me close but no one ever came. And I constantly felt degraded and desperate."

She remembered, "When I was three, my father called me 'disgusting,' and then so did my mother but I don't remember for what. Maybe because I wanted them to hold me, to reassure me that I was not disgusting."

I told Nancy, "This was the start of your feeling like a 'disgusting' leper."

She said, once again sweetly sarcastic, "And, of course, that's what you think of me now, isn't it?"

I did not reply, I wanted her on her own to gain the strength to face her early life, to realize I was not her mother or father but her analyst, someone who wanted to help her see herself more realistically. This awareness would eventually ease her pain.

I started to notice in Nancy an interesting response to my interventions, an attitude that would remain true throughout much of her treatment. When I felt I understood her, could connect her self-loathing with the past, or her distortions of my words with unempathic responses from her parents, she would claim I hated her.

This is not an uncommon response from patients. They seek to undo a sympathetic remark or a word of praise from the analyst but are not sure why. Some say, "It's too good to be true." Others, like Nancy, are deeply distrustful of the analyst, may even call him a "phoney." Many will simply ignore his attempts to be understanding.

But one afternoon Nancy changed her usual sarcasm, went so far as to say, "My previous therapists never reached the little girl in me, as you try to do. They wanted me to be a well-behaved adult. They explained what my 'adult resources' were and insisted I start using them." I felt, and communicated the feeling, that she was ready to face the child in her, yet let her lead the way, move at her own pace.

Then she returned to telling me how much I despised her. What I learned from her allowed me to understand other patients who reacted in the same way. It enabled me to help her and them feel more accepted by me and others.

One day in late fall Nancy, for about the twentieth time, told me, "You really don't like me. You are contemptuous of me. You can't stand my yearnings for you."

I pointed out, "Every time you seem to feel understood by me, you inevitably tell me how much I hate you."

She gave an uneasy laugh. "It's hard to believe anyone could really love me. Mother was too sick to love. Father was too wrapped up in himself. My brother was too competitive. My husband Paul is too egocentric. Sheila is only four years old and you can't expect love from a child who needs love."

"Apparently you'd like to believe I am a combination of all these people," I said.

Her reply would become extremely helpful to me in understanding her and other, less disturbed patients.

"If I allow myself to believe you do not judge me negatively, that you care about me, I'll become an insatiable baby," she said sincerely, even confidently. "I will want to nibble at your ear, eat it up. Claw off your nose, swallow it. Stick my head in your mouth and hold it there. And eventually, I will become one with you."

Nancy described the symbiotic wishes of a six-month-old baby, revealing fantasies she wanted to have gratified. They had never been uncovered in her previous treatments. These earliest wishes still terrified her and, rather than face them, she had buried them deep, felt loathsome for possessing them. This was what she could never express, not until she trusted me.

She was afraid she would overwhelm me with her hungry wishes and I would push her away to protect myself. I told her, "When you were a baby and wanted to be held and given to by your mother, to be one with her, unfortunately she was so sick she couldn't give much love and care. So you grew up with the idea that to want caressing and closeness was taboo."

She did not say a word but I, sitting behind her, could sense from her quiet that she was thinking about what I said. It would take a long time to penetrate the many levels of denial she had erected against facing what, to her, had been an obscene wish—to be one with her mother.

She started to share more infantile fantasies, feeling safer and safer. She spoke of a dream. "I was with a nurse whose name was Harriet but I don't remember any Harriet," she said.

She went on, "Harriet had two nurturing breasts and was ready to give me her milk all day long in my dream." Then she added sadly, "I wish you were a woman who could feed me all day. I can't stand the idea that analysis lasts for only a brief period and most of the hours of the day I am without you."

I said, "If you rearrange a few letters in the name Harriet, it would be much like Herbert. You wish I were the nursing mother you could have all day long."

I was surprised such revelations from Nancy's deepest past came during her first year of analysis. But upon reflection, I concluded she had tried so hard in her previous therapies to understand what she now told me that, with only limited encouragement, the fantasies she had wanted so desperately to discharge could easily emerge.

At one point she scared me, as I am sure she scared her previous therapists. On realizing it was safe to talk of being my infant, she regressed dramatically, started to babble baby-talk. She cooed, "Goo-ga," made other gutteral sounds, as if at the breast. A few times she called me "Mummy Herby." And once or twice announced, "I'm not going to leave your office at all. I'm going to stay with you forever."

As her desire to merge with me became stronger, she started to call me on the phone several times a day in between sessions. She left messages, some of which sounded urgent, of crisis proportion—"I can't live without you," "I'm going to fall apart unless I can talk to you," "I can't function unless I can have you on demand."

Nancy clearly was transforming me into the mother as she became the baby who wanted to be fed "on demand." As she warned me earlier, she was becoming that insatiable baby she feared she might become. She knew herself well, she realized what had kept her from growing up emotionally— the lack of proper care and love at the time she needed it most.

Suddenly there arose a very difficult period for me in Nancy's analysis. On the one hand, I wanted her to feel the freedom and safety to be herself, to share with me all her infantile wishes that up to now had terrified her, made her hate herself. On the other, to permit her to act out these wishes by calling me incessantly and trying to prolong the hour, would keep her an infant, stop her from emotionally growing and, of course, be too consuming for me personally. Her previous therapists no doubt had sensed this and had backed off in a hurry.

Although Nancy was a very attractive woman, at this point in our relationship she emerged as such a clinging baby it was difficult for me not to start feeling some of the irritation she warned I would eventually face.

I was torn between wanting to be an available and empathic parent and one who had to limit her demands. But I felt intimidated by her because I knew that any time I frustrated her she would show intense rage. However, I monitored my own anxiety as I anticipated her anger and behaved like the analyst I aspire to be.

In a session I will never forget, I told Nancy it would be best if she could tell me all she felt during her hour, not call me on the phone between sessions.

Rising from the couch indignantly, she once again regressed and lashed out. "You are the cruelest bastard I have ever met! You are one big tease. You say I should be myself but you won't *let* me be myself. I hate your miserable guts!"

Then, drawing herself up, she announced, "I am leaving therapy. I don't have to go through this torture. I'm not coming back."

She was about to walk out. I said quietly, "It would be much better to tell me all you feel on the couch instead of running away."

She stared at me as if deciding what to do. Then, grudgingly, she returned to the couch, falling upon it as though in vicious attack against an enemy. She spent the rest of the hour spewing out more invectives than I had heard from any previous patient.

"You're a monstrous, narcissistic sadist!" she charged. "If you cared for me, you'd dedicate your life to me. Instead, you're pushing me away from you. I'd like to cover your ugly face with shit, kick you in the balls. I'd like to knife you and watch you drop dead!"

Her voice was strident. She yelled so loudly and violently that Dr. Arthur Blatt, the psychologist with whom I have shared my office quarters for twenty-eight years, for the first time complained that his work with a patient had been disrupted.

While I could tell myself Nancy's rage was that of an infant being weaned, then the rage of a toddler unloved by selfish parents, I still could feel strong discomfort. I experienced myself as a bit of a villain, even though I was doing what I call "therapeutic." Nancy wanted so much to be my baby that she could not, like a baby, tolerate any frustration. I realized she wanted me to feel like a villain and take back my restraining words.

"You're asking too much of me," she said. "I've never been loved very much and now you want to take it all away."

She called me on the phone after the session, just to say, "Drop dead, you bastard," then hung up.

The wish to merge with me remained a theme throughout the entire analysis. While Nancy was able to curb her phone calls, they happened during moments of heightened vulnerability or anxiety. Weaning is never easy for any baby but seems more difficult for one who has not been fed enough love or food. Consequently, it was difficult for Nancy to accept the limits and boundaries of our relationship. I could understand why a number of psychiatrists had given up on her.

Because she somehow understood I was trying to help lessen her fear and anguish, she made some attempts to stop acting out. She talked more about her wish that I adopt her so she could be my little girl, and how angry she felt that the wish could not be gratified. She still saw my attempts at psychologically "weaning" her as rejection. She said, "If you really loved me, you would let me live with you."

She added plaintively, "Or at least let me call you any time I feel like it."

As she told me again how cruel and sadistic I was, she recalled further instances in which she felt isolated, misunderstood, neglected. One day she said accusingly, "You're trying to wean me and toilet-train me all at once."

Shortly after, she reported dreams in which she threw dirt and sand at a man in a business suit. Though her associations to these dreams consisted of wishes to play in the sand and be a spontaneous little girl, I suggested I was the man in the business suit and she wanted to shit on me.

Nancy laughed, a freer laugh than any previous one. Then she said, "That's a cute interpretation. I know I have wanted to smear your name and have told a few of my friends what a bastard you are. But I didn't realize I wanted to cover you with shit."

Allowed to be herself, she started to make up nursery rhymes in which she "shit" and "spit" and "hit" and "bit" —me.

When Nancy was not censured or criticized for her wishes to shit all over me, she began to have fantasies and dreams in which we played with mud pies and had fun getting "dirty." Slowly, perhaps for the first time in her life, she could at least tolerate the little girl within, a part of her that for so long had felt anguish and despair.

A bodily symptom she suffered for many years, unknown to me—chronic constipation—disappeared for the first time. Constipation, if not physical in origin, usually indicates the sufferer is holding back painful, unacceptable emotions that would terrify him if he became aware of them. The conflicted child, woman or man usually represses awareness of great rage at someone close, wishes to "shit" on them. He is afraid to feel his hatred because he will then be unloved, punished, perhaps annihilated.

Whenever I hear a patient complain of constipation, I ask, What emotions is he repressing? While sometimes he is holding in his feelings of sadness or grief, more often the predominant emotion is revenge. This was certainly true of Nancy.

She induced in me the feeling I was bringing up a child. Earlier during this phase of treatment, she had been what analysts call an "oral" baby. Later, she became an "anal" toddler. She began, toward the winter months, to become more of the "oedipal," sexy little girl of three or four.

One day, after thanking me for weathering many psychic storms with her and declaring I was "different" from her previous therapists, she described a dream in which she danced with a gray-haired man who wore glasses, describing him as "a professional type." With only mild encouragement, she talked of her wish "to dance" with me. She fantasied us "making good time and sweet music with each other."

I recalled a comment offered by one teacher in my early years of analytic training: "Dancing is a vertical expression of horizontal desires." This approximated a saying I heard in adolescence that described dancing as "a navel encounter without the loss of semen."

Nancy was showing progress, proving once again that a caring therapist who can see a schizophrenic patient and himself as quite similar, can help the patient face his inner self.

But as soon as I started to enjoy her progress and maturation, Nancy would have to undo it. She could fantasy dancing with me and having sex with me, then abruptly turn me into a villain out to kill her.

She reported one fantasy in which she visualized my penis inside her, then said, "You enjoyed it but I felt exploited and humiliated." She accused, "You look too pleased with yourself these days. I feel you have conquered me. You strut around like a big cock-of-the-walk and I hate your guts. What pleasure is in it for me?"

She spoke as though she felt very sexual whereas in reality she was extremely fearful of sex. Her husband was the first man with whom she permitted any sexual intimacy, she admitted, though she always enjoyed sexual fantasies.

That she was still enmeshed in infantile thoughts about sex became evident. She spoke of wanting to "eat me up," "rip off my penis," "merge" with me, engage in sadistic-masochistic whipping. Several times she announced, "I want to urinate on you and have you do the same with me." When a child feels this way, he is presenting his urine as a gift, asking for the same gift in return. At an early stage in life we believe our urine a precious, coveted substance, to be bestowed only on those we love.

The early power of these fantasies had immobilized

Nancy in her realistic sexual life so all she was capable of, before marriage, was to be a "good friend" to men. She was terrified to act as a sexual partner lest she indulge in her childhood fantasies.

Nancy never had sex with a woman but, she admitted, she enjoyed sexual fantasies about women. She often pictured herself sucking at the breast of mother figures. She also thought at times about "going down" on a woman, licking her clitoris and, in turn, allowing the woman to do the same to her. She also imagined herself possessing a penis and "fucking women hard," her fantasy of being the powerful male.

As Nancy complained how much I was exploiting, manipulating, seducing her to gratify my sexual desires, I realized how exploited she must have felt by her father when he took care of her medical problems as a child. It occurred to me that he probably touched her naked body at times seeking knowledge of her ailments and this would have been sexually stimulating to a little girl. It would also have proved very upsetting after her mother's death, when Nancy's main rival for her father's love no longer stood as barrier against the oedipal taboo.

I received confirmation of this when in one session she said, "You are a molester." It was as though she wished me (the father figure) to become a molester, since now her mother had vanished forever.

"Will you explain exactly how I molest you?" I asked.

"You force sex, in which I have no interest, upon me," she said. "You place me in a hypnotic spell that makes me feel I want to dance with you. But you can't let me just dance. You want to rape me, get me to spread my legs for you."

Again here was the fantasy-wish that her father have sex with her.

With contempt in her voice, she accused, "You're a male whore. I pay you money to get help and instead you enjoy your sexual kicks." Then confirming my thoughts, she added, "At least my father didn't charge me when he took my temperature rectally. Or examined my body for sores. Or massaged me when I told him a part of me hurt. But you want to use your cock as a tool to injure me."

She kept repeating the phrase "You want to injure me." During a moment when she seemed less angry, more reflective, I asked, "What comes to mind about how I injure you?"

She said, "My father would sometimes hurt me when he took my temperature by sticking the thermometer up my behind. I felt excited at his touch so I didn't mind the hurt too much."

Inserting a thermometer up her rear end was tantamount to inserting a penis in her vagina, Freud would have concluded. This "displacement" of the site of the hurtful (but wished-for) sexual act connoted physical contact with her father.

She went on, "I even liked it when my father lanced a boil, though that hurt, too."

This was her first reference to suffering from "boils," a painful infection and its equally painful cure. The lancing of her boils would have created many fearful and sadistic wishes to inflict the same pain on the one who caused it.

"I remember when my father would burst my boils, so they wouldn't fester and infect me. I was frightened to death

I would die—not from the boils but from the knife he used to open them up."

I thought, as a little girl, she imagined her father wanted to kill her by pricking open the boils with a knife, perhaps to avenge the death of his wife, which Nancy believed she had caused.

The lancing of the boils may have been the start of her fear of being murdered. In her fantasy, her father may have been her first assailant, bent on dealing death. But I would wait before offering this interpretation. I would rather hear it from her, that she believed her father, the doctor, wanted to kill her with a knife when, in reality, he was relieving her pain. I thought of the knife she used on her own body when I went on vacation, as if she was telling me of her earlier fears.

Nancy confessed: "I felt one way I could bring my father closer to me was by being sick. I don't know to this day when I'm really ill or faking it. If I complained something hurt, my father would stop everything to take care of my body. As though he was its master."

This caused a split in her thinking. She could draw him closer only if she was in pain. Her feelings were split—to be loved, she had to be sick.

She recalled further, "After my mother died, I produced aches and pains at night. My father would rub my legs and my back. Sometimes I slept in the same bed until the pain went away."

Sleeping in the same bed meant fantasies of sexual closeness to her father. She would feel aroused, at the age of six and seven, and then not only unable to sleep but guilty. Her desire would remain unfulfilled and, because of its intensity, cause overwhelming frustration.

Her father had never remarried and I wondered about the depth of his emotional involvement with his daughter. Perhaps some day I would know more details. I would have to hear them from Nancy. She would need to remember and then reveal them if I were to accept a too-deep and damaging emotional, or even bodily, relationship between her father and her as anything but my fantasy.

4

THE

SEXUAL

EXPLOSION

Winter 1980–81

As winter approached, it grew dark outside the windows of my office during Nancy's hour. Then the first heavy snow of the year fell in December, the tenth month I had seen Nancy. She arrived in an ankle-length mink coat and hat. Even her boots were trimmed with fur.

I was pleased with her progress. At times I even wondered if she had been misdiagnosed. Often psychiatrists and other mental health professionals, in their irritation with hard-to-control patients—intense, anxious and emotional—handle their hostility by branding the patient "psychotic." True, Nancy had shown in her initial interview with me intense paranoia. And later, her sudden shift from ordinary calm to furious rage revealed a departure from reality. But much of the time she appeared rational and willing slowly, sometimes painfully, to explore the analytic path that led to a lessening of her anguish.

She told me more than once that the opportunity to talk to me as I quietly listened, seated behind her, was in sharp and happy contrast to the attacks on mind and body she experienced in the mental hospitals. This also afforded her a new freedom from the isolation that had characterized so much of her previous "help."

She proved something I experienced occasionally with less severely disturbed schizophrenic patients, and which pioneers in the treatment of schizophrenia emphasized—*the therapist's humane attitude and conviction that the very disturbed patient is "more human than otherwise" enables the patient slowly to feel and act "normal."*

If a person is treated in the rather cruel fashion that has traditionally characterized care of the schizophrenic, he starts to lose what self-respect and trust he may possess. He becomes more isolated, more regressed, feels more violent. This, in turn, convinces the psychiatrist that indeed the patient is subhuman and that analysis is a waste of time.

A different picture emerges if we equate the schizophrenic patient with the vulnerable, injured child who needs patience rather than punishment, concern rather than indifference, warmth and acceptance rather than coldness and rejection. Children love the adult who gives them these emotional nutrients. The adult then feels loved by the child and a mutually enjoyable, constructive relationship ensues. I saw Nancy as a combination of younger sister and daughter who needed, among other things, brotherly support and fatherly understanding.

Nancy sensed the genuine feelings in me that keyed my professional behavior. I treated her as if she were a member of my family and, in turn, she began to respond with appreciation and cooperation. She trusted me more and more deeply.

Hallucinations and delusions are expressions of despair from someone who finds reality terrorizing and unbearable. They are no longer needed when he acquires a relationship in reality that provides the nurturance and gratification that strengthen a stronger sense of self.

As I worked with Nancy I became convinced that the more a schizophrenic patient is involved in a compassionate human relationship, the less he needs to produce hallucinations, delusions and other psychotic symptoms, such as the loss of the ability to speak "sanely." Just as all of us daydream and fantasy when life appears frustrating, the more vulnerable person, one we label "schizophrenic," daydreams more desperately and fantasies more intensely. What is a daydream to a "normal" person becomes a nightmare in the day-to-day life of the schizophrenic child, man or woman.

It was not magic or unusual therapeutic interventions

that helped Nancy appear more whole, more "mentally healthy." She thrived on the constant reassurance of my concern, hope and genuine acceptance.

At this time in Nancy's therapy I recalled perhaps my most creative contribution to the professional literature. I discovered in the early 1970s, while a professor at Rutgers University, that the best therapists for in-patient schizophrenic patients are first-year social work students. I had reviewed over fifty cases in which such students helped schizophrenic patients to leave hospitals and experience a fuller life. How did this come about?

These students did not know what schizophrenia was—their ignorance was their greatest asset. Rather than worry about "pathological narcissism," "immature ego functions," "severely impaired object relations," "punitive superegos" and "incapacity for therapeutic alliance," they related to their patients as fellow human beings in distress whom they wished to understand and help.

I was particularly struck by the fact that many of these students were not sophisticated intellectually. Frequently they had great difficulty conceptualizing psychotherapy and psychopathology. Yet they achieved such positive results with patients that my research project was written up in several professional journals, sponsored by psychiatrists belonging to the American Psychiatric Association.

To confirm my perception that Nancy was starting to feel more human, she now told me that she felt warmer toward her husband. During one session in late December 1980, she said, "The icicles on your window remind me of how frigid I've been with Paul. But I should tell you that during the last month we resumed sex for the first time in a year."

Nancy still did not talk much about her husband and daughter. She felt too overwhelmed by her own conflicts. Now she started to express her feelings about Paul and Sheila. She loved her daughter, but at times Sheila, as all children do, disobeyed her mother's wishes and Nancy punished her by ordering her to go to her room, close the door, and forfeit supper. Sheila would hurl looks of hatred at her mother, slam the door as she retreated into her room. Nancy would always relent, bring food to Sheila's room even before her own supper was served. But sparks of hatred sometimes flew between mother and daughter.

In an addition to their usual routine, once in a while Nancy would invite for dinner a fellow teacher and her husband, or visit their home on a Saturday evening. She told me she had made two new friends recently among the teachers.

I reflected on how Paul coped with Nancy's schizophrenia. Like most spouses of schizophrenics, he appeared to vacillate between extreme anger and occasional empathy. Much of the time, from what I could surmise, he seemed to feel hidden anguish, desperation and hatred. This mirrored in many ways her more overt anguish, desperation and hatred.

Just as Nancy often expressed hatred of him, as though he was her teasing father, ungiving mother or competitive brother, Paul treated her as though she was one of his difficult parents, as if his own parents had environmentally programmed him to mate with someone as difficult as Nancy, someone most like themselves. Although I did not know much about his past, I knew enough to realize he was far from a happy person when he married Nancy—he, too, had his neurotic reasons for marrying.

One of the things of which analysts are certain is that only happy people make happy marriages. It is impossible to conceive of a happy, mature man or woman marrying a schizophrenic man or woman. Analysis has shown that spouses are inevitably at the same level of emotional maturity as the one they chose as mate. While their overt behavior may differ, in that one may be sadistic and the other masochistic, or one is an alcoholic and the other tries to halt such behavior, each sees himself in the other person—often not consciously but vicariously.

Paul showed in a more disguised way than Nancy deep infantile wishes for love. He suppressed a strong rage. His wishes went unfulfilled and a need to suffer emerged because he felt so guilty for his rage. She had related how, when she first met him and revealed her stays in mental hospitals, he had wanted to rescue her from what he called a "cruel world." This attracted her to him, for he was the rescuer she had long sought and she loved him for that. Thus he knew how emotionally disturbed she was before they married, but his wish to rescue her was powerful enough to cloud his reason.

Anyone who wishes to rescue others, as Paul did, also wants to *be* rescued. His attempts at therapy however were short-lived, probably because he was too afraid to face his buried rage, which therapy inevitably would have uncovered. Like most people who shun psychotherapy, Paul was too frightened to face the pain self-revelations inevitably prompt.

I noted that many men and women in analysis feel their

emotional plight is one of "everlasting punishment," as Nancy did. Recently I walked past the corner church to my office early in the morning, after parking the car and noticed the announcement of two forthcoming sermons. One was on "Everlasting Punishment," the other, "Testimonies of Healing." I thought of how analysis is an attempt to "heal" a mind that "punishes" itself everlastingly and that just as medicine attempts to heal bodily wounds, psychoanalysis attempts to heal wounds of the psyche.

I was pleased to hear both of Nancy's social life with her husband and her expanding sexual desires, but was careful to monitor my enthusiasm. I knew she felt throughout most of her life that she had to "put out" for her father and other men. It was important for her to feel she enjoyed sex for herself, not just to please her husband or her analyst "father."

Thus, when she told me of her new progress, I said only, "Oh." I was trying to express acceptance without elation, understanding without approval.

But even my neutral "oh" was too much for a masochistic personality like Nancy. She said sarcastically, "I bet you feel smug and triumphant now that you've persuaded me to screw more often."

Then she said accusingly, "Like all Freudian shrinks, you want to make me into a sexpot and then you feel like a ballsy big shot."

Her choice of denigrating language, as well as her rage, showed how she had to debase sex and derogate me. It was almost as if she was a reluctant virgin I had used to enhance my power. She was showing me this was how she frequently felt with both her father and brother, and sometimes her husband—as if she was the butt of their hostile gratification.

For many weeks Nancy derided me time and again. She charged, "You don't care one whit about me. This analysis is all for you. And that's what sex is like with Paul. It's all for him."

At another point she commented: "I'm positive that you, my father, my brother and my husband, care more about your lousy cocks than you do about my soul."

I was later to remember these words, of great significance to her. She felt sexually exploited by her father and psychologically demeaned by her brother. This was clear. While her language was at times obscene, it left no doubt as to what she felt.

Nancy hoped I would fight back, kept trying to provoke me into arguments. She wanted to arouse my rage, create in me an anger comparable to hers so she would not feel she was the "bad girl" and I, "the good guy."

One day she asked, "Can you prove you have any interest in me besides making money and feeling like the cock-of-the-walk? Can you show me that you are any different from my arrogant father?"

When I did not argue or defend myself she became even more exasperated. She seemed eager to start a fight, showed deep frustration when she realized I would not respond. She went so far as to tell me, "You made a mistake in expecting me to go through the tortures of submitting to sex with Paul as often as he wants it."

She added sullenly, "Masturbation is good enough for me. I don't want any more children."

Then she challenged, "Why don't you admit you made a mistake? Come on. Say it—or I'll leave at once."

She started to rise from the couch, waving a fist at me.

"It would be much better if you could tell me how much you resent me, rather than ostracize me," I said quietly.

Reluctantly, she fell back on the couch. "You always want to be on top, to make me submit."

I asked, "Is that how you feel when you have sex? Always on the bottom, exploited? Never really enjoying it?"

She started to sob. I learned early in my career never to interrupt patients when they cry. It is equivalent to stopping someone in mid-orgasm.

I waited until Nancy's tears subsided. Then I asked, "What were you thinking as you became so upset?"

Articulate, emotive Nancy said, "I drew a blank. I had no thoughts."

Then she sighed, went on, "I guess I felt all alone. As if you weren't in the room. It reminded me of the many lonely hours I spent in my room as a child, when I felt afraid, very afraid. There was no one to go to for comfort."

Something within Nancy then caused her to retreat into silence—a long silence. One that lasted, unbelievably, almost two months. She ignored all my attempts to persuade her to speak. Perhaps this was how she felt when a child in need of comfort, I thought.

I realized that just as she withdrew from her husband and refused at times to give in to sex, she had now withdrawn from me, not wishing to give herself to the exchange of words. Perhaps talking on the couch was similar, in her fantasy, to sex, and she was saying she was damned if she would give me that gratification.

Although all patients occasionally retreat into silence, it is only the very agitated, disturbed ones who regress into a long, pure silence. Most express a deep yearning to talk and be understood. While all feel resentful at moments, few stop talking completely.

And so I had to ask myself, Why does Nancy come to her sessions on time, head for the couch and then spend weeks not saying a word? She gave me little opportunity to help, other than to say from time to time, hoping to spark a response, "You resent talking to me." Or, "What's the difficulty in talking?" She still said not a word.

I felt quite frustrated at her long stretch of silence. I wanted her to talk. It was the only way she would feel relieved. Yet I also knew this was a woman who, all her life, felt pushed and pressured to produce for others. If I tried too hard to persuade her to talk, she would only feel more controlled, more misunderstood, more rageful.

Despite my discomfort, I knew it was more important for Nancy to uncover the mystery of her sudden silence. Why should anyone seek a psychoanalyst's help, pay over several hundred dollars to lie on the couch forty-five minutes four times a week and say nothing?

What was the mystery of her silence? I kept asking myself. Since she now seemed the last person in the world who would tell me directly, my only recourse was to free-associate during those silent hours and discover what my own thoughts yielded.

I believed Nancy still must be obtaining some satisfaction from coming to my office. Perhaps she wanted me to be the one who felt impotent and rejected. Just as she would not at times let her husband stimulate his penis in sex, perhaps she wanted to render me a flaccid analyst. I told myself, She wants me to feel as helpless, as weak, as desolate as she feels.

Yes, there is a teasing, tormenting quality to this silence, she *must* want me to suffer, I reasoned. Nancy is in no mood to corroborate my hypothesis and I am in no mood to ask if my thoughts make sense. Then I recalled that after trying to persuade her to speak, and realizing it was a futile fight, I had said, "It's fairly clear to me that you do not want to talk. So I will join you in your silence and when and if you are ready to talk, please feel free to do so."

But after almost a month of complete silence, I dared ask in the middle of a wordless session, "How is it going?"

I expected further silence but, to my astonishment, she said with moderate contempt, "The analysis is really great. For once in my life I don't have to put out for a soul. And you accept this. You haven't thrown me out, or punished me." Then she hid once more behind her wall of silence.

I almost fell off my chair in amazement. I felt uncomfortable hearing Nancy call her analysis "great," while I sat quietly, offering not a word. It was like earning an "A" on a difficult examination without cracking a book, or receiving a raise without working for it. I felt quite guilty.

Then I received a telephone call from her husband, his first contact with me, which made me feel guiltier. He told me in a deep, grateful voice, "Dr. Strean, you are a miracle worker. For the last three or four weeks Nancy has behaved

like a sexually aroused woman. We are enjoying much pleasure in bed. I want to thank you."

I had expected him to complain that Nancy was paying
vast sums of money for empty hours. Instead, those empty
hours had somehow achieved a break-through for her in a
very important psychic area.

Paul thanked me further by referring his friends to me
as patients. They all reported he had given me "rave reviews,"
which further compounded my guilt. I felt uncomfortable receiving referrals and accolades for no apparent reason. At no
time in my psychoanalytic training had I learned doing and
saying nothing would achieve such heartening therapeutic
results.

It soon became clear that as long as Nancy could use
me as the target of her hatred and resistance, she felt free to
enjoy Paul and understand—and accede to—his emotional
and sexual needs. The more she could discharge her hatred
toward me, the more she could feel freer to relate warmly to
Paul. Were it not for my presence on the scene, Paul would
have continued to be the target of Nancy's childish hatred
toward her father, brother and all men.

Most analysts explain such behavior as stemming from
a child's deeply ambivalent feelings toward a parent, feelings
that become "split" in adult life. Many a married man or
woman hates a spouse but loves a paramour. I have also seen
the opposite, where some hate their lover, thus enabling them
to feel free to love their spouse. They fantasy the world is
filled with "good" and "bad" people. They do not realize they
are expressing long-buried childhood hate toward a parent.

Thus I could infer Nancy was expressing her hatred for

me by her refusal to speak to me. This freed her to express her sexual desire for Paul. I obviously stood for her forbidden father. Were it not for my presence on the scene, Paul would be the target of her oedipal love—as he had been.

I could surmise that Nancy both loved and hated her father with a passion. If she had just hated him, she would have left me and also Paul. And if she had loved him far more than she hated him, she could enjoy a warm, tender relationship with Paul and me—perhaps not even have needed therapy.

But no child is exempt from ambivalent feelings toward parents. Nancy, like every child, was tortured to some degree by feelings of hatred and feelings of love, though her feelings were so intense that eventually they had destroyed her ability to take much pleasure in life.

As I reflected on Nancy's teasing me through silence, I noticed as she lay on the couch, she frequently lifted her skirt, only to hastily swirl it back into place. She also occasionally moved her body seductively, as though enticing me to join her. It became clear she was trying to arouse me sexually.

I said to myself, This is what her father probably did to her. His silent presence must have aroused her sexually, stimulated her desire without giving or accepting fulfillment —unless this was a case of incest, which I doubted. Her father sounded like quite a moralistic man, though why he never remarried was part of the puzzle.

I could guess that his rage at his wife for dying so early in their marriage, leaving him with two helpless children, was great. I also suspected that he probably had poor mothering and would be wary of marrying again. Perhaps visualizing himself as sole parent seemed easier than bringing a strange woman into the house. He probably was unaware that by not remarrying, he had placed a special burden on his daughter, who fantasied herself as his new wife.

Men and women who have enjoyed fairly loving marriages, then lose a spouse to death, are likely to marry again. Most do not feel overwhelming guilt when they seek another sexual partner. But very often those who have endured an unhappy marriage will feel guilt if they search for another mate, as though the former spouse is still "in the bedroom."

The fact that so many married couples refer to each other as "mommy" or "daddy" proves that in their unconscious, the spouse becomes the childhood mother or father. The oedipus conflict has not been fully resolved so the fantasy may recede and the mate recognized as a person in his own right.

I could only assume that Nancy, at this moment on the couch, was doing unto me what had been done unto her. To some extent her father may have been both violently and sexually aggressive toward her, then withdrawn. Nancy's later behavior was graphically described by Anna Freud as "identification with the aggressor." Many children abused violently or sexually later assume the role of the one in power. They emulate the exploitative parent rather than the sorry victim they feel themselves to be.

The child who has undergone a tonsillectomy at the hands of a doctor who "hurts," after he feels better often persuades his mother to buy him a stethoscope or tongue depressor. He then plays the doctor, pretending to take out the tonsils of other children as he reenacts a past trauma, now the one in control.

I still could not share any of these thoughts with Nancy, I had to keep respecting her silence. Finally in February 1981, a moment I still vividly remember, she broke her silence.

Suddenly she turned her head toward me, blurted out, "Why don't you get off your stupid rump and help me?"

I felt slightly shocked at the contrast between Nancy's all-encompassing silence that dominated our recent sessions and the sudden intensity of her anger. I waited for her to say more.

She started to vilify and condemn me once again. "You really don't give one hoot about me. All you're interested in is accepting my money and taking care of yourself." Her tone combined exasperation at and contempt for me, plus a certain resignation as she said, "You're such an inadequate man but what can I do about it?"

I knew she unconsciously was attacking the father of her childhood, who had been both father and mother. Because she had been silent for almost two months, it was important for me to keep quiet. This would permit her to discharge the fury she had held back. At this point in treatment, just short of a year, she did not need much encouragement to describe what a dastardly human being she thought I was. I possessed the analytic awareness not to take it personally, as I did when I first started training.

She charged, "You just sit in silence, hour after hour, probably thinking of everyone else in the world except me. Don't you realize I'm a very needy person? Don't you sense

I am furious at you because I need your help desperately and you are failing me? Don't you know all my life I've hungered for someone to love me and have always been disappointed?"

Slowly Nancy's hatred was dissolving from its emotionally stoney prison. She started to reveal, as is frequently the case with someone who hates intensely, that she desperately wished to be given to, taken care of, but found this too terrifying to verbalize.

She experienced me both as the uncaring mother who died and deserted her and the cold, seductive father. She was convinced I could not be compassionate because I was similar to both parents—feeble, like the mother she hardly knew and exploitative, like the father who undoubtedly used her unconsciously in disguised ways as the target of his pent-up sexual feelings. In addition to fearing any response from me, even though she demanded it, Nancy felt her yearnings for love and caring were too overwhelming ever to be fulfilled.

Over the next few months she started to accept the fact that I would never censor her for her rage—a fact it is difficult for almost all patients to accept because their parents would not allow them to express anger (only the parent was permitted to do this).

Nancy now revealed what she really wanted from me— a nurturing, symbiotic, loving mother, a warm, compassionate father and a sexually satisfying lover. All these wishes had been repressed over the years, just as a dam holds back the powerful rush of water that seeks release. Nancy's yearnings had been imprisoned in her unconscious for three decades but were now given my permission to be released—in words only.

The yearnings now gushed forth like explosive geysers. She shouted, "Goddamn it! Why the hell do you have to sit behind me all the time when you know I want you to lay on the couch beside me?"

This had been her wish when she charged, "Why don't you get off your stupid rump and help me?" By "helping," she really (unrealistically) meant "gratify me sexually."

In the following session I said, "It will help you if you tell me what your sexual fantasies are when you picture me on the couch beside you."

Nancy responded, "Bullshit! Why should I picture it? Just lie down beside me."

When I did not accede to her plea, she begged in a far-softer voice, "I really need you. I want you desperately. You have to come inside me. I feel empty without you. I would feel so good close to you. I want you to be my Siamese twin. Never leave me."

Then she said assertively, "I am positive that if you lived with me and had sex with me all the time, I would never feel any aches or pains. Life would be perfect."

Silence, then, "We would always be able to talk and agree about everything. There'd be no fights."

I now learned one of Nancy's most dreaded vulnerabilities. She said, "If you ever disagreed with me, I'd feel dead. If you agreed with me, I'd feel alive. When Paul and I go to the theater and he likes a play I think is poor, I feel he is rejecting me. You and I would always agree. We'd be perfect lovers, one person, not two."

Nancy would refer quite often to this wish for oneness, in terms of Siamese twins and of the Biblical characters Ruth and Naomi, blood relatives, who told each other, "Whither thou goest, I will go." Nancy said, "Where thou liest, I will lie," meaning on the same bed.

While the description of being one applied to two romantic lovers, Nancy really wanted me to be a symbiotic mother—a mother to whom she was literally tied, the umbilical cord uncut. One of her dreams at this time clearly spelled this out.

"I was in bed with you having sex," she said. "It was very fulfilling and exciting. Your penis swelled up bigger and bigger until it was wrapped around my whole body. You roped me in." She gave a soft laugh of pleasure.

"Tell me your thoughts about being 'roped in.'"

"It's like your penis became an umbilical cord," she said. "I was tied to you—you, the cock-of-the-walk!"

I realized something to which I had been insensitive as a young psychoanalyst. Nancy's passionate desire for me was not merely the wish of a sexually hungry woman for a man. It revealed her equally, if not stronger wishes for the love and care never received from a mother or father. Her words, "I was tied to you," express how a baby feels the first months of his life toward his mother.

I said, "Your wish to live with me is strong not only because you would like me to be the perfect man you have fantasied but also the perfect mother you have needed so desperately."

She at once corroborated my interpretation with tears, agitation and a certain excitement, as though discovering a new psychic truth. She said, "I've always wanted a perfect mother and a perfect father but every time I wished this I thought of myself as an ugly-looking leper who didn't deserve perfect parents."

There was silence, then: "For the first time in my life I am beginning to feel I am not such a horrible person for wanting to be showered with attention."

The outrageous demands we all make of our parents in childhood have to be consciously faced before we may think more maturely of ourselves and others, I thought. I was grateful Nancy had taken this gigantic psychic step.

In the next few sessions she went back and forth between talking about her wishes to be my "one and only" and to be the "one and only" in her family, thus, in fantasy, killing off her rival brother. She recalled childhood dreams of lying in the same bed with her mother and father as they became "one happy family."

Nancy then mentioned her night terrors as a child. She said she would often awake from a dream feeling a wolf had been chasing her and she could not run because of acute pain in her legs. I realized these were disguised wishes for her father, the doctor, who in reality rubbed her legs when they hurt. He was also in her fantasy the wolf who chased her and who, she wished, would subdue her either violently or sexually.

She displayed more inner ease after speaking of intense, childhood longings. She was now able, for the first time in treatment, to show interest in her obvious rival on the current scene—my wife. Nancy started to ask questions about her, repeated them in subsequent sessions. I, of course, did not reveal a single fact but encouraged her to fantasy what my wife looked like and what kind of relationship she had with me, which would tell me more about Nancy.

She said wistfully at one session, "Your wife must be a warm and loving woman who takes good care of you." But she soon revealed her deeper fantasies when she blurted out, "I really feel very angry whenever I think about your wife. I want you all to myself. I resent every hour she spends with you."

Then she added sarcastically, "I suppose, compared to her, you think of me as a second-class citizen. Not as pretty, not as bright, not as sexy and not as giving."

Nancy now felt like the little oedipal girl of four or five. She fantasied my wife as her rival mother, wanting her father—me—all to herself and her mother dead and gone.

I suggested, "You want my wife out of the picture. Permanently."

She replied, with confidence, "I feel if I play my cards correctly I can get her out of the way and possess you completely."

This, of course, was exactly what occurred in her early life when her mother died. Nancy then had her father completely to herself. She did not question his never considering remarrying.

Suddenly, instead of addressing me as "Doctor Strean" or "Doctor" or "Strean"—the latter used when she raged at me—Nancy suddenly started to call me "Herb," as though we were indeed married.

"You and I are sympatico, Herb," she announced one sleety afternoon in early March. "I know the way to your heart. I'm attuned to your unconscious as you are to mine. I am sure we could marry and live happily ever after."

Then she added, in an acidic way, "But I would worry about your poor wife being the loser."

Almost all patients express this desire to do in my wife but few feel so entitled to gratify their fantasy. An analyst's wife is experienced as the good mother and/or the exciting lover. Women patients want to take her place and men patients wish to be the recipient of this "perfect" woman's nurturing and sexual desire. I was surprised at how confident someone as emotionally disturbed as Nancy appeared as she described our living together as husband and wife in perpetual bliss. Then I remembered Nancy had always been her father's little "princess."

This early belief that she could easily take her father from her ailing mother had served to cause overwhelming guilt when her mother actually died. If a child loses the parent of the same sex, the loss becomes an oedipal, but a forbidden, triumph, for incest is our strongest taboo. The child feels swamped with guilt. He believes his death-wish has killed the parent who was his rival, as in the ancient Greek story of Oedipus. The child feels both grandiose and guilty.

It was important, I knew, to help Nancy experience the intensity of all her wishes—the wish to enjoy a blissful sexual and symbiotic relationship with her father and the wish as a child that her mother die so she could possess her father. If Nancy could accept as natural her death wishes toward her mother, she would feel far less guilt, far less depression, far less need to punish herself.

Her self-image would be not that of a murderer but of a child whose fantasies resembled those of all children. A child naturally wishes to marry the parent of the opposite sex as preparation for choosing an appropriate mate when the time comes for a mature love relationship.

Nancy suffered, as do all patients who remain very infantile, from her grandiose fantasies—fantasies she was not about to give up quickly. She kept reiterating, "You should take pity on someone who suffers as much as I do and have sex with me. You should become my lover and friend rather than my therapist. You should be available on call."

After realizing I would not respond to her pleas and demands for sexual gratification, she started to complain about me steadily. She accused, "You don't appreciate what a wonderful woman I am and how much better off you'd be with me instead of your wife."

She brought in vivid dreams that she interpreted. "I burned down your house last night and your wife and children unfortunately died but I saved you." She described another dream with the words, "I was in a 'Miss America' pageant and you were the judge. You chose me as Miss America. You and I then sneered at all the other women."

As she became more and more aware I would never succumb to her erotic wishes, she constantly demeaned my wife, my female colleagues and my other women patients. She described sadistic fantasies toward all of them. I listened, did not judge. I knew Nancy heaped severe emotional abuse on herself for her murderous feelings and needed to air the fantasies that whirled within them. Only by releasing the fantasies to awareness could she accept them, be free of her damning guilt.

Love and hate are our two most powerful emotions. If we do not make peace with our hatreds somewhere along the road of life, it is difficult to find love.

P A R

T II
THE
SECOND
YEAR

SPRING
1981

5

AN UNFORGETTABLE DEATH

Spring 1981

Nancy had survived her first full year of analysis. April brought to Central Park, stark and bare during winter, a new flowering of trees and bushes. But to Nancy, the external beauty meant little or nothing as she described fantasies in which my wife was murdered, usually by an unknown villain wielding an ax or knife.

I believed, as I have said, that in general the patient who

has been hospitalized is not that different than those able to live comfortably on the outside. At times I have found myself saying to students and colleagues, "The whole world is a mental hospital. There are the in-patients and the out-patients and often it is difficult to know who's who."

All children have death wishes toward parents or rivals. For the child who has been emotionally abused or neglected, these feelings are more intense, create more havoc in his mind. The very disturbed person defends desperately against his forbidden wishes. The extreme example is the catatonic schizophrenic who withdraws completely, refuses to utter a word lest he be driven to commit murder. He imagines the mere articulation of the thought of murder as no different than the act—the wish automatically ensures that the monstrous deed is done. This is the small child's fantasy.

There are three types of schizophrenic patients—the catatonic; the "simple" schizophrenic who regresses in an extreme way, speaking and acting like a little child, sometimes appearing nonsensical and peculiar; and, like Nancy, there is the "paranoid" schizophrenic. He projects his violent wishes onto others and fears being attacked, even executed, because of the mammoth guilt that follows on his wrath.

As Nancy expressed more and more of her buried hatred toward my wife and my other women patients, she felt less angry and vituperative. But now feelings of depression set in. She spoke of loneliness, recalled times as a child and adolescent when she felt completely abandoned.

It became clear that through her dreams and fantasies of wishing my wife and other women dead, she was starting in depth to relive her mother's death. This trauma would consume many analytic sessions because of its devastating effect on her at the time and during all the following years.

In one session she kept insisting, "You must do something for me."

I asked, "What would you like from me?"

She replied in all seriousness, "I'd like a cup of coffee. No, I'd like a glass of milk. No, I'd like a breast that holds milk. Yes, that's what I'd like—a mother who could feed me milk."

Suddenly she regressed as far as any patient ever had on my couch. She turned into a gurgling baby, demanded, "Milk, milk, milk! I want milk, milk, milk."

She then called me "Mummy Herby," saying, "Mummy Herby will give me milk, milk, milk."

After several such declarations, she fell into silence. I said, "If I become a good mummy and give you my breast and milk, I will be very much alive—unlike your dead mother."

Nancy lifted her head abruptly from the couch, turned around and looked directly at me with startled eyes. She exclaimed, "My mother's not dead! She's here in this room. You're my mother. You're not dead. I didn't kill you!"

How did Nancy deal with the fact that she could act very emotionally disturbed at times yet was aware of such overreactions? This is a question often asked when I report on my work with schizophrenic patients. While there exists some variation from patient to patient, I have concluded that a psychotic episode, when reflected on by someone like Nancy, is experienced in much the same way that most of us experience a nightmare.

When we wake from a nightmare we tend to view it as something that happened *to* us—often as an experience imposed on us by a mysterious force rather than one we conjure for ourselves. The average person tends to view most of his dreams as stemming from something he ate or other external factors. The schizophrenic patient tends to view his psychotic episodes similarly. But just as psychoanalysis can prove to the average patient that his dreams are the "royal road to the unconscious," as Freud called them, and help the patient discover how he arranges to be his own worst enemy, someone who works with schizophrenics can do the same thing. He will help a patient like Nancy understand why she needed to regress to the point where she really believed I was "Mummy Herby."

All of us—psychotic or not—regress to infantile forms of behavior when our current reality becomes too oppressive. The more painful reality seems, the further we regress into childhood fantasies. We need to regress at times because reality can never be completely gratifying but how *far* we regress depends on how devastating is our current life. For instance, colleges are aware that graduates need at times to return "to the good old days" and visit their "alma mater" (loving mother).

For Nancy to be a mature, sexual woman meant she had to face her still active childhood wish that her mother was dead—in her child's mind, this meant she had killed her mother. It also meant she could now be the "lover" of her father—a dangerous thought. But if she made me "Mummy Herby," her mother was still alive in me, I could not then also be her lover. She no longer however would have to worry about her murderous wishes.

If we look at schizophrenia as an attempt to regress to primitive modes of feeling and behavior because current life is too tormenting, or appears like a losing battle, then the ranting and ravings of patients confined to mental hospitals become far more intelligible. The patient shows there *is* "a method in his madness."

"Mummy Herby" was Nancy's way of saying: "I cannot cope with my oedipal conflict. You are too inviting a father figure and it would make me feel as if I was murdering your wife if I gave in to my love for you. But if I make you Mummy Herby I do not have to worry about sexual fantasies toward you as a father. And I do not have to worry about getting rid of a mommy because *you* are my mommy, right here in this room."

Her behavior this session was quite quixotic. Like all schizophrenic patients, she distorted and denied reality because it loomed as too devastating. She believed in the hidden part of her mind that she had killed her mother but found this thought totally unbearable. It was unacceptable to her conscious mind. Most children repress the wish for their parent's death—even the most punitive and vicious parent imaginable, one who commits incest or beats the child regularly.

But if the parent dies and the child has felt deep hatred because the parent has brutalized and terrorized the child, he becomes convinced he is a murderer. This was one of the main causes of Nancy's furious flight from reality.

Every child has fantasies of omnipotence. He wants what he wants when he wants it. This wish follows all of us to the grave. No one, not even the best-analyzed psychoanalyst, is exempt from the omnipotent wishes of childhood. Most of us learn to tame these wishes, accept them as belonging to childhood. But if omnipotent wishes remain too strongly entrenched, block out reality, then the child, or the adult, begins to think, "Maybe I can run the universe."

If we understand the patient in the mental hospital as suffering from childhood omnipotent wishes he wants to gratify, even though he feels terrorized by them, then we know why it is common for the hospitalized schizophrenic to claim, "I am the Emperor Napoleon." Or, "I am God." Or, "I am Jesus." Or, like Nancy: "I can have you, psychoanalyst, as my mate and kill your wife off because I am a princess."

This childhood omnipotence was brilliantly described by Lewis Carroll in the acts of the Red Queen. When she did not like someone, even a stranger she hardly knew, she would order, "Off with his head!" Carroll's work is dedicated to the omnipotence of childhood, one reason children (and the child in the adult) love it.

Most of us have our needs gratified at least to some extent the first few months of life, all babies feel omnipotent. But sooner or later reality intrudes. Mother is not available pronto. The diaper is not immediately changed when wet. Aches and pains persist without instant relief. Yet if the environment is a fairly loving one, the child slowly gives up his omnipotence, though not without protest.

Usually, if not always, most children for some period

think of their parents as omnipotent. Freud pointed out the more helpless we are—and as children we are always helpless to some degree—the more we need and want an omnipotent parent. Freud believed it was out of our helplessness that we turn to religion and ask support from "our father who art in heaven."

If the environment is a hateful, hurtful one so that the child becomes in reality helpless, cannot rely on his parents for emotional support, then he may resort to a feeling of grandiose omnipotence and fantasy he is king, queen, God, whoever. Or he may withdraw from life, like the babies Dr. René Spitz wrote about. They had no mothers, were placed in hospitals, and gave up wanting to live, died.

I told Nancy, "You hate yourself so much because you think of yourself as a powerful child murderer."

She responded quite candidly. "I know you're trying to help me feel less tortured and less guilty. But I still really believe I killed my mother."

I wondered if this fantasy was the underlying one in schizophrenia—incorporating both the wish to kill because the parent somehow was seen as cruel by the child and the belief he was the murderer, as seen in Nancy's case.

Referring to Nancy's iron-clad belief in her own omnipotence, I asked, "I wonder why you persist in looking at yourself as so powerful that your wishes could kill?"

Her response was one I had encountered many times in patients, although in my first years as a therapist I was always surprised. She said in astonishment, "You mean I'm not *that* powerful? I didn't kill my mother? I'm just a weak slob? A helpless child?"

She then added indignantly, "You're trying to take my power from me!"

I learned once again that it is difficult for a patient to give up his long-entrenched feelings of omnipotence—even though the feelings cause acute suffering. The alternative in Nancy's case was to view herself as a helpless, weak, vulnerable child who could influence nobody—not only a denial of what she believed the truth but also a giving-up on life, which equated with death.

One day I communicated this thought to Nancy: "If you don't make yourself a powerful murderer in fantasy, you feel like a nobody."

She corroborated my interpretation with memories in which she felt like a "nobody." She recalled that at the times her mother fell ill, she fantasied herself either as mothering her mother or killing her out of anger at her mother's seeming ignoring of her.

The month of May moved in quietly, and I hoped that the rainstorms of April had been left behind. During one session Nancy said in a thoughtful tone, "My mother's death could occupy a whole book. I have much to say about it that I have not as yet told you. I've only, in essence, described a few chapter titles."

Then she asked in a scarcely audible voice, "Is it all right with you if I spend some time telling you about a book I might write called *My Mother's Death*? I still feel responsible for her dying. I feel somehow I should have been able to save her."

I hoped one day Nancy would accept that she had nothing to do with her mother's death. The wish is not the deed.

But no amount of reassurance or consolation helps a severely guilt-ridden patient. When you tell emotionally tortured men or women they are murderers in fantasy only, they look at you as if you are an idiot. Every therapist who works with even mildly neurotic patients learns that the guiltier the person feels, the more he believes he is an accursed, actual criminal.

Such was Nancy's plight. She realized, in one part of her mind, that her mother had suffered from cancer, remained in bed for nearly two years as doctors visited the house, then died. But despite Nancy's intelligence and, at times, fairly solid grasp of reality, she believed she was a "leper," a "hateful person." It took me many years as an analyst to realize that when someone believes an untruth with passion, this serves a vital psychic purpose.

It was my task to find out why Nancy *wanted* to believe she had murdered her mother. I say "wanted" because no one had ever accused her of such a crime. Only she called herself a killer. In spite of the fact psychiatrists and other therapists had told her otherwise, she held tenaciously to this conviction.

She confessed to me now, as if stating a fact, "I killed my mother. There's no doubt in my mind."

I knew there was nothing I could say to change her fantasy. She would have to find out for herself, after she faced enough of her terrifying wishes, that she was innocent.

I had to help Nancy understand that just because she had wished her ineffectual mother dead did not mean she murdered her. I thought of the many practitioners and scholars who claimed that because the schizophrenic patient has never successfully gone through the oedipal stage of development (but remains "fixated" at the infantile "pre-oedipal" stage), he is incapable of mastering his wish to kill the parent of the same sex and marry the parent of the opposite sex.

This incorrect view of the schizophrenic patient becomes a self-fulfilling prophesy. If the therapist believes that the schizophrenic patient has not been able to go through the normal stages of development, albeit with trauma, then the patient will be viewed as someone "fixated at the oral stage, he has never traversed the anal and phallic-oedipal stages of development."

If the therapist views the patient as a completely and exclusively regressed infant, then he will not even consider helping the patient resolve murderous fantasies toward the parent of the same sex. The therapist will see the patient as doomed to helplessness. After a while, the patient also will be convinced of his sorry state. Such reaction has been noted over and over in many fields. For example, if teachers view students as "stupid" or "uneducable," the students respond as "stupid" and "uneducable."

I strongly believed that Nancy, like all of us, experienced the fantasies of an infant at the breast as well as the trials of a two-year-old who had to learn to urinate and defecate in the toilet. But in addition I viewed her as a sexual human being. Very few psychiatrists acknowledge the schizophrenic patient's sexuality, or believe he is capable of love, close relationships or enjoyable sex. (I wonder if this reflects the psychiatrist's own fear of sexual intimacy.) At times therapists act out this biased view not only with schizophrenic patients but also with less emotionally disturbed men and women. Thus the patients never achieve loving relationships.

By the time I saw Nancy, I had worked with many children who lost a parent during the oedipal period of development. In a 1961 paper, "Mothers and Sons in the Absence of the Father," I reviewed my clinical experience and that of other therapists. All of us pointed to the inescapable inference that virtually any child whose same-sex parent dies during the oedipal stage, inevitably believes he is the killer. The well-known child analyst Dr. Peter Neubauer stated this in his paper "The One Parent Child and His Oedipal Development," published in *The Psychoanalytic Study of the Child*.

Every so often my wife kept appearing in Nancy's dreams and daydreams. Though Nancy had referred to her occasionally, she now occupied a prominent place in this psychoanalytic stage of Nancy's dramatic and traumatic life.

One afternoon Nancy remarked, "I dreamed that your wife was my superior at school. She told me how to get along better with children, how to enjoy smoother relationships with them."

I thought her interest in my wife now represented the wish for a mother to nurture and love her as her own mother was not able to do. Paralleling this hypothesis, Nancy associated to the dream: "I always wanted a mother who would tell me about the facts of life and help me become a good mother. I guess that's what I'd like your wife to do."

While this desire for the nurturing, benign mother was one of Nancy's wishes, when I asked her to free-associate to the thought that my wife would be her supervisor, this translated into "overseer" as Nancy reluctantly said, "I guess I meant your wife is the bossy type."

The following week she reported, "I dreamed last night I became one of the bosses of my school. I was head teacher and the principal and I were finally pals, not enemies."

Nancy was able to talk about her ambition to advance professionally but she was not able, without my help, to understand that in the dream she made *me* the principal. I said, "I think you would like to take over my wife's job and be my pal."

She did not agree with my interpretation. She said scornfully and angrily, "I would never qualify to be your pal."

There was a moment of silence, then she explained in a more controlled voice, "I'm sure I am one of your least favorite patients. I've been told that most of the women you see in analysis are therapists who study at your psychoanalytic institute. These women are your harem and they admire you. You know damn well you love it. I'm only a teacher, a second-class citizen. I do not qualify as your 'pal.' "

I kept quiet, wanting her to go on. She recalled, "I felt the same way with my father and his women patients. He often left me out of his life because he spent so much time with them. This was an everyday occurrence as I grew up because his office was part of our house but even so, he was always late for supper."

I suspected, because Nancy's gynecologist father had direct contact with his patients' bodies, particularly with their sexual parts, that his patients early became formidable opponents in her imagination. She must have felt like a "second-class citizen" next to the stream of nubile ladies who came to the house—this lonely girl terrorized by the absence of a mother.

After I listened carefully to the account of her extreme jealousy of her father's patients, I said, "Your father spent so much time with women patients I would think that what you wanted to be more than anything else *was* a patient." I wondered, Could this be one reason she wound up as a patient in five mental hospitals?

She exclaimed with delight and relief, but also with considerable agitation, "Yes! You hit the nail on the head! I remember often rushing to my father to ask him to examine my body for one ailment after another—itchy back, sore throat, earache, irritated rear end.

"You're saying I wanted my father to examine my body, too? That I wanted to feel as important to him as his patients?"

I added, "And wanted him to touch your body and admire it."

She admitted, "I hated my father's patients. He gave them so much time, care, and devotion. My mother was his patient too before she died. There was little affection left for me."

I pointed out, "Just as you viewed your father's patients and your mother as women he cared about—more than he cared about you—this is what you seem to be doing with my wife and my other women patients. You make them your superiors."

Much to my surprise, she did not object to this interpretation but said quietly, "I guess that is why I made your wife the school supervisor in my dream. I feel she is superior to me."

As Nancy could focus on her competition with my wife and women patients, she recalled more of her hidden resentment toward her mother for occupying so much of her father's time, as well as her resentment toward his patients.

She recounted a dream in which one of the children in her class blurted out, "I didn't do it! I didn't do it!" She was speaking for herself, for in a dream we play the part of all the characters—they each represent some fantasy or wish.

Then Nancy talked of students in her class who "always tried to get away with things," and of her daughter Sheila, "who tries to get away with murder behind my back."

I asked, "What did you try to get away with in your childhood?"

For the first time in several months, Nancy abruptly retreated into a psychotic state. I had asked, without realizing the drastic reaction it might cause, a psychically charged question.

She screamed, "You dirty bastard! You're trying to trick me into admitting a crime! You think I'm a criminal, don't you? This analysis is a lot of shit. I hate your guts. You keep trying to force me into admitting something I never did!"

As is true of all dreams, the child in her dream was the child in her adult self, repressed in her unconscious. Nancy was the child who kept insisting, "I didn't do it, I didn't do it!"

Nancy was suffering from a primitive conscience, or as we analysts say, an "archaic superego," which constantly told her, "You're a murderer. You're a murderer!" a self-accusation characteristic of many criminals with the strong wish to commit murder, driven by a fury they cannot control.

When someone suffers from this strong a conscience, he rarely views the conscience as his own. Rather, as in a nightmare, he feels the conscience as some external force that doles out severe punishment to him. Many times the very guilt-ridden person wants to get rid of the punitive voices he hears and may wish to kill someone he believes his enemy. This is one reason why some very mentally disturbed patients have tried to kill or have killed their therapist. They believe their own punitive voices are the therapist's and that he forced his voice on them.

Intelligent, capable and articulate, Nancy felt guilty about her hostile fantasies focusing on her absent mother and teasing father. She felt the punitive voices resided outside her—with the principal, occasionally with her husband and intermittently with me. She had to attack all of us from time to time as she made us her punitive conscience.

A person who possesses such a strong conscience needs help in accepting the fact that he has suffered emotional abuse in childhood. The anger still lies within and if he can understand it is no longer necessary, that he now has control over his life, it will diminish. This task of facing and accepting buried anger is vital for everyone in analytic therapy and, to a degree, for all of us. As I have said, no parent is perfect and every child will at times feel abused. We have to realize our guilt comes from within, not from without and that to reduce it, we have to face and understand our hate.

From everything I could determine, though Nancy as

far as I know was never subjected to overt incest, I am convinced that what transpired emotionally between her and her father had dire consequences on her adult life. He also examined her frequently when she complained of pain, sometimes "injected" needles and medicine into her or dropped pills in her mouth. Like any girl whose father touches her body, no matter if his purpose is medicinal, Nancy became highly stimulated and excited. Yet, as she once said ruefully, perhaps also referring to me, "He offered his carrot but he didn't give me much of a nibble."

As she grew up she felt sexually stimulated and deeply frustrated. It gave her the impression *she* was perverse, wanting gratification but feeling it was always withheld.

As I compared my work with Nancy to other women who suffered incestuous attacks, I thought that in some ways the young daughter who is tormented and teased is left with deeper psychic pain than the girl who has suffered actual incest. The latter usually can feel a righteous degree of rage toward a father who realistically exploited her, she does not have to feel she is "perverted." While each girl who has been sexually abused by a father reacts in her own idiosyncratic way, I am inclined to believe sexual teasing and the emotional pain and frustration it brings leads to a more tormented mind.

Nancy's father occasionally had dates with women a few years after his wife's death but they were never serious, she said. Without consciously realizing it, he used Nancy as a substitute for his lost wife, rather than treating her as a daughter. That she would even dare marry, I thought, attested to her inner strength as she obviously went against her father's wish that she never leave him.

Yet she was not able to lose the powerful belief she had killed her mother. She experienced me as her primitive conscience (or superego) that accused her of murder as she defended herself, "I didn't do it!"

Her adamant attitude as well as her powerful paranoia made me wonder if my question, "What did you try to get away with in childhood?" had been too strong, appeared too early in treatment. As I scolded myself for asking it, I became aware of something that frequently occurs in psychotherapy, particularly in the treatment of the severely disturbed patient.

I was becoming like Nancy, berating myself, trying to convince myself I was not really so destructive—I had not made such a bad mistake. As I analyzed my reaction—blaming myself for being too harsh on her, trying to convince myself I had not been too harsh—I realized I was experiencing precisely what Nancy was experiencing. She felt she had killed her mother, blamed herself for murderous feelings and acts even as she tried to convince herself she was innocent.

As I studied my reaction even more carefully, I recalled both childhood and adult dreams and fantasies about aggressive, resentful thoughts toward my mother and father. I remembered a childhood dream at six in which I turned my father into Hitler, who marched in to seize me from my home and deport me to a concentration camp. I also recalled times my mother threatened to evict me from the house because she thought I acted too belligerently.

As I reflected on these hostile memories I could empathize with Nancy's hatred toward her parents. I recognized, too, how guilty she felt because of them. It was never easy for me to confess to my analyst how much I felt at war with my parents. In many ways, as I confessed this, I felt like a real delinquent, even in part like a Nazi. I gained from my personal analysis the awareness that whenever I felt deep hatred, it always indicated feelings of weakness and vulnerability. I learned the most effective way to diminish hatred and increase love is to come to terms with what makes us feel weak and vulnerable, or with what Dr. Karen Horney described as the root of all anxiety, "feeling like a lost child in a hostile world."

One day in late May 1981, Nancy told me, "A fellow teacher is very sick with a bad heart condition." This was a woman Nancy liked and admired. After visiting her friend, Nancy shared her feelings with me.

"When I saw Elizabeth lying there sick, weak and vulnerable, I admit part of me said, 'There but for the grace of God go I. Thank God, I'm alive and well.' I guess I felt a bit smug, superior to Elizabeth. I could keep on teaching while she prepared for the grave."

Then Nancy suddenly became very agitated. She bellowed, "You goddamned bastard, you. You're a persecutor. You're trying to get me to admit I murdered my mother. That I want to murder your wife. And that I'm out to murder Elizabeth, another rival."

I kept silent, wanting her to release and face her rage. She obliged, spit out the words, "I don't know why you're so intent on destroying me when I've had such an unhappy life."

For several sessions she continued to make me her punitive, hostile conscience that wished to punish her for murderous, competitive fantasies. I remained silent as she tried with all her might to taunt me into flagellating her for her angry feelings.

Finally she demanded sarcastically, "Why don't you defend yourself? Why don't you deny you're out to get me? Just get off your stupid rump. Do your job."

I said quietly, "You want me to fight with you, argue with you. Will that make you feel sufficiently punished?"

She scoffed, "You're trying to act like the neutral analyst who doesn't punish his patients for murdering their mothers. You know damn well you hate me for standing by and watching my mother die. Somehow I should have saved her."

She added, a catch in her throat, "I really wanted to help her but I didn't know how."

I was moved by Nancy's statement that she wished to help her mother. I thought, What could a six-year-old do to cure cancer? Because of her natural childhood feelings of omnipotence, Nancy thought she miraculously could have kept her mother alive but, because of her oedipal feelings, instead fantasized she was her mother's killer.

The next session she came in with a dream in which she appeared as Madame Marie Curie, the woman who studied the medical application of radium. Nancy said, "In the dream I felt a sense of power, as if I could save the world." She added helplessly, "I couldn't even save my mother."

"You felt it was your task to keep your mother alive. And you've been punishing yourself needlessly ever since her death. It was the doctors who couldn't save her. She was too ill," I explained.

Tears started to stream down Nancy's pale face. She

asked, in a little-girl voice, "Wasn't it my job to stop her from dying? Shouldn't I *somehow* have prevented her death?"

"There was no way you could have," I assured her.

I thought once again, in awe, of the omnipotent power all children assign to themselves. They think they are God or the devil. Only as we mature do we realize we are neither—we are merely human, prone to err at times, far from the perfect self that would assure us our parents' total love.

Nancy now recalled the many times during the period of her mother's illness that she went through obsessive and compulsive rituals. She prayed endlessly, touched dolls for good luck, as though they could help prevent her mother's death. She promised God she would forever after be a "good girl." But when her mother died, she became in her own mind the reverse, an entirely "bad girl."

Once more she called herself a "leper," saw herself as sadistic, cruel, mean. She wailed, "I aided and abetted my mother's death."

By mid June, Central Park was now thick with the foliage of trees and the fragrance of summer flowers. Nancy said something she would repeat many times. She uttered the words sadly. "I'm nobody without a mother." This meant that because she felt she had murdered her mother, she was not entitled to live.

She told me, "As my mother lay dying, I became more and more numb. As I saw less life in her, I felt less life, less air and blood within. I had no right to live if she didn't live."

At that point in her life Nancy would have benefited from a therapist's help, though there may have been no outward signs of her need. Her gynecologist father certainly was unaware of her acute inner distress. Perhaps even if he had been aware, he would not have permitted her to see a psychoanalyst or child therapist.

I told Nancy once again to reassure her, "You never had the power to kill your mother. This was a childish fantasy."

From my limited view in the chair behind her, I saw her hands fly upward as she said, elated, "You're saying I'm not that powerful? That this was my illusion?

"To this day, I often have fantasies of being Wonder Woman, a superagent, an associate of God in heaven. Something in me wants power very badly."

She added, rage in her voice, "I suddenly feel angry at you because you're pointing out that I never was nor could I ever be powerful."

Although this was the same reaction she showed a few months before, she now seemed to have more conviction. She needed to feel strong, I thought, because she felt so weak, because she had been so destroyed by whatever emotional, perhaps also physical cruelties that had been inflicted by her mother and father in her early years.

Nancy was telling me that by revealing the fantasy of omnipotence and the unreal part it played in her adult life, I had exposed her "evil" thoughts to the bright light of reason and they were no longer "evil." She was starting to sense also that she was not the "Wonder Woman" she fantasied herself to be. While part of her resented this as reducing her to a mere nothing, another part, the rational part, started to accept the devastating price she had paid for ignoring reality.

It would take Nancy a long time before she could look at herself as a "human" being. Not a "Wonder Woman" who could kill and destroy her enemies at will.

All of us possess this feeling to some degree but most of us face it consciously as adults, accept it as illusion. In Nancy's life very early severe traumas forced her to maintain the illusion, as though it was vital to her psychic life since her own reality was too terrifying.

I had to ask myself, Was it the early death of her mother, so devastating to a child? Or were there other, equally traumatic experiences, perhaps at the hands of her father, brother or a stranger that shattered her right to enjoy a life free from her heavy burden of emotional pain?

My analytic intuition told me there must be other factors in addition to her mother's death. Seldom, if ever, is it only "one" cause when the mind is this deeply affected. Nancy's five breakdowns, her deep hatred of herself and everyone else, must have been precipitated by other traumas.

Analysis is much like playing detective and searching for clues but with one difference—the patient has to provide the clues to what is called his "soul murder."

6
THE
LITTLE
PRINCESS

Fall
1981

Nancy was not quite as upset during her second summer break from analysis as she had been the previous year. But, like all patients, she viewed my absence in terms of how she felt psychologically.

Just before vacation she spoke again of "feeling like a nobody, as though I am without a mother or anyone who cares." I told her a month ahead of time I would be away during August and after a few attempts to ward off the reality that she would be alone for a month, she announced, "Without you, I am nothing. Ever since the beginning of the analysis I feel my worst the days I don't see you. If I had you with me all the time, I'd feel more like living."

I was reminded once again of the difference between the neurotic, whose emotional attachment to the early mother has been far less damaging, and the psychotic, crippled because he never has been able to break free of the early ties to the mother and develop a strong sense of independence. Because of her mother's early death and, no doubt, her mother's incapacity while alive to help her young daughter, Nancy had failed to mature emotionally in a healthy way, even though she managed to marry and bear a child.

The neurotic only dreams of the terrors that haunt him, whereas the psychotic believes the terrors are real. He lives as though his wildest fears exist not in his imagination but are part of his working life.

Nancy now called me "heartless" once again. She attacked me continually, accused me, as she did before the first vacation: "If you really loved me and were a kind and considerate analyst, you'd take me on vacation with you. Freud saw his patients when he went on vacation and there are therapists in this country who do the same."

She added, "Or, if you weren't such a goddamned, narcissistic bastard, you'd stay in New York and see me."

Nancy then spent a number of sessions alternately bombarding me with accusations of selfishness or pleading with me not to take a vacation or at least to let her go along. Then suddenly, with two weeks to go, she became extremely solicitous, offered to do favors, clean the waiting room, dust my floor-to-ceiling bookcases, decorate my office suite in a different style.

As is necessary with all patients, I asked her to subject her wishes to thoughtful examination rather than gratify them. When I did not say "no" or "yes" to her offers, she exclaimed, "There's no way of getting near you, is there?, you cold, calculating scientist."

At least "scientist" was an improvement on "bastard," I thought, grateful for small changes.

She added, "Sometimes when I wonder what you look like as I lie here on the couch, the image of a skeleton comes to mind."

She was now wishing me dead. Her feelings of gratitude had vanished.

I asked, "What thoughts do you have about my being a corpse?"

"You offer so little warmth, so little kindness, so little human emotion, how could I consider you anything but a corpse?" she said scathingly.

She was, of course, talking about the real corpse in her early life—her mother. She then recalled a dream in which she rose from the couch, walked over to my chair and saw me "on the verge of dying."

"You are experiencing me as a skeleton, a corpse and someone on the verge of death," I said. "What do you suppose this is all about?"

She responded without hesitation, "When I saw my mother dying I hoped that if I did her favors, maybe she would live. I guess that's why I offered to fix up your office, take care of you. Because I really don't want you to go on vacation and leave me all alone."

Somehow Nancy survived the summer reasonably well. She returned to analysis in early September with only mild-to-moderate resentment about my forsaking her for a few weeks. She did not harm herself—no slashed stomach as in the previous year. She even showed a fair amount of enthusiasm on resuming analysis.

In her first session she said, "I started to read more of Freud's work when you were away. I guess it was my way of keeping you near me. A few times I thought it could have been you talking as I absorbed what he said."

She also mentioned that during August she suggested to colleagues at her school that they seek a psychoanalyst. And she discussed with Paul the possibility he try therapy.

It became clear Nancy felt more secure, experienced more self-esteem and calm as I compared her reaction this fall to my vacation the previous year. The first time we separated she had plunged into an agitated, suicidal state. Now she championed psychoanalysis, allied me with its founder, Sigmund Freud, whom she respected and admired. She wanted her husband and friends to benefit, as well as herself, from Freud's important discoveries of how the mind works, both consciously and unconsciously.

Like all patients and human beings, when Nancy could love she felt more joy in living, more sense of an esteemed self. When consumed with hatred, as during the previous August, she thought life worthless, literally wished to die.

I recalled Freud's famous statement: "People fall ill when they cannot love."

I also remembered a corollary that came from my analyst, Dr. Reuben Fine: "Much of analysis is helping the patient reduce his hatred. As he is able to do this, his neurotic problems diminish."

This does not mean we stop feeling angry when frustrated, or irked when provoked. But it does mean some of the intense wishes for revenge against parents and others who have hurt us have been faced and dissipated. Such wishes, if not accepted, will keep us emotional cripples and prevent us from assuming control of our thoughts and acts.

In addition to reading Freud, Nancy tried to discover more about my personal and professional life. She told me one day toward the end of September, "I see you're a big shot at the New York Center for Psychoanalytic Training. Maybe I'll take a course there. I hear they allow teachers to take their courses."

Then, shyly, she asked, "Will you admit me?"

This was a loaded question, one fraught with sexual connotations. She wanted to know if I would accept her in my analytic community. "Admitting" her was psychologically equivalent to responding to her wishes to be close to me. If I said she could take a course, she would feel blissful. If I denied her, she would experience this as hurtful rejection.

I now had the fantasy of Nancy sitting in a class I taught and emerging as an articulate and brilliant student. As I analyzed this fantasy, I realized it came from a wish that had never been gratified—to have a daughter after two sons. The last thing an analyst consciously wants to do is to use his patients to release his own frustrations. I had to monitor my wish to have Nancy as a student—and daughter—and therefore could not permit her to take a course with me. Over the years I have learned a great deal about my own "counter-transference."

Consequently, I was only moderately surprised, after asking Nancy to describe what came to mind about taking courses at my Institute, to hear her ask, "Don't you realize I'd like to be your daughter?"

She went on, "If I took a class with you, I could feel fed intellectually and stimulated to think more deeply."

I thought, And mothered and fathered.

As she associated further to taking a course, she developed as powerful an erotic transference as perhaps I have ever witnessed in a patient. Although she had already made sexual demands in the previous year and she had also described in fantasy several sexual encounters, now, in October 1981, Nancy seemed totally determined to be my lover, my daughter, my comrade, my colleague.

She described dreams and fantasies in which we did everything from enjoying romantic candlelight dinners to erotic sex in hotel bedrooms of Paris, Rome and Honolulu. She placed us in more sexual positions than I can honestly remember.

She also told me how much she would enjoy reading poetry to me and listening to me read to her, as well as going to the theater and "psychoanalyzing the themes of the plays."

Her erotic wishes and desires for a loving relationship were somewhat different from most patients in that she did not look at her desires as fantasies, the way the less disturbed patient does. She became extremely demanding, wanted an immediate response from me.

"Enough of this talk," she said in a November session. "I want action. I'm sick and tired of conducting mental masturbation with you. I'm disgusted with all this mind-fucking. I don't need therapy. I need a human relationship."

Then she begged, "Will you stop teasing me and give me what I need?" She threatened, "If you don't, you'll regret it because I will commit suicide."

She went on in even more ominous tone, "I am *not* kidding. This is no idle threat. You know I've tried suicide several times. I've been in comas and nearly died. If you don't stop this teasing, I will leave a note saying it is all your fault."

While patients have made threats over the years, this was as intense a one as I had ever heard. Furthermore, I believed her. She truly felt that if I rejected her sexually she did not wish to live.

This represented how she felt toward her father—she had never worked through the strong oedipal conflict we all face, starting at the age of four or five. At this time we naturally become attracted to the parent of the opposite sex in preparation for the later capacity to choose a proper stranger as, we hope, our lifelong mate.

But even though aware of Nancy's "transference" love, my heart beat ever more quickly as I heard her threats. I felt a combination of many feelings. Stimulated, because this attractive woman desired me so deeply. Frustrated, because I knew I would never even shake hands with her. Angry, because she was trying to manipulate me.

Her shrill voice and intense demanding attitude also brought to the surface a feeling I had as a boy with my own hysterical, at times, mother. It was as if my mother now threatened me, "Herby, do what I say or you'll be in deep trouble!"

Nancy's threats reminded me particularly of a stage in my pre-adolescent life when my mother threatened to send me to an institution for delinquent boys if I did not heed her admonitions. Nancy was threatening to send me to some imaginary "institution for incompetent psychoanalysts."

As I reviewed what I felt, which always dissipates tension, I started to think once again of where Nancy stood psychologically and why her demands seemed much more intense than those of any other patient with whom I had worked over the previous three and a half decades.

Nancy had spent many years alone with her father after her mother died. Her father never sought a second wife and Nancy felt, I was quite sure, like a replacement for her mother, now minus a brake on her strong oedipal feelings. Though she resented the many responsibilities hurled at her, she clearly felt she was more than "Daddy's little girl."

She undoubtedly made claims on her father that the average little girl of seven and eight dared not make in the presence of her mother, even though she might think them, wish them to become true. Without a mother present, the claims could in fantasy grow to horrendous proportions, unfulfilled though they might be.

One of the problems I have seen in children who live alone with the opposite-sex parent is that they tend to become pathologically narcissistic. They feel as though *they* were the parent's mate now the obstacle—their hated rival—is out of the way. Nancy talked in her fantasies of being my "mate" as we traveled from Rome to Honolulu, shared the same bed, or as we attended theater in Manhattan.

I realized that what I had to do for Nancy was to help her be less of a demanding infant and child, one who felt she had every right in the world to wish to sexually possess me as she wished to possess her father. She had to become able to accept normal frustrations, rejection and the realities of life. The latter included the fact that her father had belonged sexually to her mother and that her analyst must analyze only, never become an actual participant in her fantasy of desire.

In one session, Nancy repeated, for at least the tenth time, "You *must* come over to the couch this minute and lie down with me, right now!"

I said, after taking a deep breath and trying to sound more relaxed than I felt, "When you become very demanding of me sexually, what goes on inside you?"

To my amazement, she suddenly leaped from the couch. She stood in front of me, stared at me with as vicious a sneer as I had ever seen on the face of anyone. Then she snarled, "What a stupid, idiotic, crazy, unfeeling son-of-a-bitch you are!"

She was silent a moment, then hurled out the words, "Asking me what's going on, when what I need is to be loved! That's like asking a bleeding child, 'Why do you want a bandage?' "

For the following two sessions she continued to vilify and condemn me. She told me over and over, "You encourage me to be myself and when I am, you slap me in the face."

She then insisted, "Now I *am* convinced you hate me and want me to commit suicide." She added plaintively, "I don't know why you hate me so much. If you loved me, as I think sometimes you pretend to do, you'd be my lover. Or my friend, at least. But all you do is hold out a verbal carrot and when I try to take a bite you say, 'No, no, little girl.' "

I repeated her words, "Little girl?"

She said, with loathing, "Yes, you bastard. You treat me like a little girl. You put me on a couch, stir me up sexually, make me want you and then say, 'You're just a little girl.' "

Nancy then told me that when she thought of the "carrot" I held out but never gave her, she would "love to bite it— hard!" She added, "That's what I'd like to do to your stiff cock. Bite it and eat it so you'd never see it again. Then you couldn't dangle it in front of me."

One of the most refreshing aspects of working with Nancy was that she, like most schizophrenic patients, did not defend against forbidden fantasies and wishes as the less disturbed patient on the couch does. To talk of "biting off" the analyst's penis is very difficult for the average analytic patient, even though he is encouraged to speak of everything that comes to mind. The only "sin" in analysis is holding your tongue because you do not want to reveal an act or thought you believe will lower the analyst's opinion of you.

When a schizophrenic patient, like Nancy, enters psychoanalytic treatment, he speaks as a child without showing the usual restraints of a neurotic patient. One of the first clues analysts receive to the schizophrenic process is the highly violent or vulgar language that is used—phrases like "biting off your cock," "I want to kill you," "let's screw." Nancy readily maligned me with a primitive verbal sadism.

The fantasies that a less disturbed patient reveals are exaggerated in the hallucinations and delusions of the schizophrenic. The neurotic patient will say, "I'm worried you don't like me." The schizophrenic will say, as Nancy did, "I know you hate me and want to destroy me." The neurotic will say, "I am afraid you'll reject me." The schizophrenic will aver, "You want to poison me, kill me." Sometimes these differences may be subtle, difficult to differentiate, depending on the degree of the illness.

Early in my career I discovered that regardless of how distorted and convoluted a patient's utterances, he needs to feel that I take him very seriously and am trying to understand his conflicts and ease his inner pain. I have noticed in my work, and in the work of psychotherapists and psychoanalysts I have supervised, that if the patient, regardless of the words that pour out of him in rage or self-pity, is not censored or squelched, he inevitably begins to recall pertinent memories that spark his feelings and fantasies.

When patients are genuinely accepted, no matter what their feelings toward the analyst, they inevitably begin to understand they distort the present, make it a replica of their tormenting past. To recognize why this occurs, the analyst must accept whatever the patient feels in the present—otherwise he will never help the patient ease his psychic pain.

That I could be at times fond of an unlikable woman is part of the treatment of a schizophrenic. There is always much that is unlovable about a severely emotionally disturbed person. In a case like Nancy's, the analyst has to examine himself, find out why he may at times respond with impatience and anger, as undoubtedly the parents did. Many mental health professionals also do this, using the patient as a therapeutic scapegoat as they inflict electroshock and endless drugs, some of which prove dangerous to the health of the patient.

Often the hallucinations and delusions of a disturbed patient who has been labeled a full-blown schizophrenic are heightened when he is not understood, as happens too often in mental hospitals. Nancy knew I was trying to understand her, and her sense of self-esteem, what therapists call "ego functions," started to emerge when she could talk of buried feelings. This made me feel even more strongly that schizophrenia is not a biological disease. Select any depressed person and allow him to talk to you and he will feel less depressed.

When I first started as a psychoanalyst, I was uncomfortable with a patient's pronouncement of love for me. I would prematurely tell him that he wished me to be his mother and father. He would at once feel rejected and, in several instances, would promptly leave treatment. Soon I realized that "falling in love" is quite subjective, that the phrase has its irrational components and relates to childhood. Yet no one who feels he is falling in love wishes to believe for one second that his feelings have irrational roots in the past. To tell Nancy that love for the analyst was in reality a carryover of the love she felt for her father would have seemed like a slap in the face. She had to discover for herself the source of such a wish—she would not have accepted my explanation.

Thus when Nancy told me I made her feel like a child who was sexually and emotionally "teased," I did not deny her perception but asked, "Could you describe more of your thoughts about me?"

A few weeks later I queried, "Could you tell me why I seem so sadistic?" A word she often used to describe me.

As she heard the word "sadistic," she started to cry. After drying her tears she said, "What I am feeling with you seems very familiar."

The word "familiar" comes from the word "family." She proceeded to recall experiences as a young girl within her family that revealed feelings and fantasies that proved important as sources of her present emotional disturbances.

She had referred a few times to sex play as a child between herself and her brother. She also mentioned, as though in passing, her mixed feelings when her physician father touched her body after she complained of aches and pains. I felt she was ready to tell me more, and, indeed, she was.

She said wistfully, "I often felt like my father's little princess. After a hard day, he would sit on the sofa beside me and tell me all his troubles with patients. He would explain what a hysterectomy was and appendicitis, if the woman had to have her appendix removed."

Then Nancy added, as though she felt it not quite proper, "Sometimes he would put his arm around me and hold me close. Then I felt even more as if he belonged to me."

There were other confessions. "From time to time we'd talk about my little brother as if he was our child. This was exciting to me."

After she made the powerful admission that she fantasied being her father's wife, she suddenly became withdrawn. For the first time in treatment she appeared late, then seemed in a hurry to end the session. This was new behavior. I wondered if we had approached too swiftly some of the deep danger zones in her emotional life.

In December 1981, as the pattern continued, I said, "You've been moving away from me. Do you have any thoughts about this?"

She replied defensively, "*You're* moving away from *me*! You don't seem as interested as you did at first."

Then she said in a calmer tone, "You'd think after all I told you about my father and me, you'd have more to say. Instead, you just sit there. All you want to do is *understand* me. You're a very unresponsive lover."

I knew this reproach was meant for the father of her childhood, who would go just so far, then retreat. He would touch her when she complained of pain, hold her close on the sofa after a hard day's work with his patients, then refuse to go "all the way." A child tantalized sexually considers this acute rejection. Nancy in her fantasy thought of me as the abandoning lover of childhood, not as a psychoanalyst who wished to free her of destructive fears and wishes that had deeply warped her ability to attain a mature form of love.

She brought in several dreams in which she chopped off my head, castrated me, threatened to kill me, substantiating my thoughts. In one dream she told me she did not know whether the man she was trying to destroy was her father or me.

"Perhaps I am treating you in a way that reminds you of your father," I said.

She exclaimed, as though I had struck a psychic gold mine, "You're both teasers! You both make me feel you love me and then withdraw your love. Sometimes when I got a boil near my vagina, my father would feel around down there. I would quiver with excitement."

She fell silent, then in calmer voice said, "I yearned for him to touch me inside, to rub my clitoris, to give me an orgasm."

Another silence, then: "You know what that coward would do? He would withdraw his finger, leave me hanging, unfulfilled. Do you know what torture that is? No, you don't! Men don't understand how a woman feels when they arouse her and then walk away."

She added, almost in a mutter, "Sometimes Paul has that problem. He comes too fast and leaves me in agony. Once, after he fell asleep, I masturbated and thought, 'I can do it myself, you creep. I don't need you.' "

Her voice rose in anger. "And that's just what happens here when you say at the end of a session, 'We have to stop now.' "

She was so furious she turned on the couch, sat up, looked at me, then screamed, "You and my father and my husband! Three teasing bastards!"

I thought, Good for Nancy, she is starting to reach for the early trauma in her life—trauma so severe it had crippled her natural capacity to work through emotionally the sensitive, complex attachment to her father, an attachment every little girl experiences and, hopefully, makes peace with as she matures.

The tragic early death of Nancy's mother and the fact her father did not remarry, led me to conjecture that he wanted Nancy to remain his "little princess," impaled on her desire for him. He unconsciously wished to infantilize her, so she would stay chained to his side.

He may have believed his ministrations to her body were necessary for her physical well-being, unaware of the sexual arousal they produced. He showed, however, that he did not want his "little princess" to grow up and leave him for another man, as proved by his failure to select another wife, a more appropriate object of his sexual love.

As I thought of Nancy's relationship to her father, what seemed to upset her the most was what she experienced as sexual "teasing." When she complained she suffered pain, her father would touch her bare skin, which stimulated her sexually. He then left her "high and dry," as she put it.

In sexual stimulation of the kind Nancy experienced, the child does not know what to feel. On the one hand, when there is teasing, the child becomes sexually aroused. The parent may or may not feel guilty, depending on his depth of awareness that what he does is very harmful to the child. The child, who feels omnipotent, will blame himself, does not think of himself as victim.

This emotional chaos, which starts as excessive stimulation and ends with painful frustration, leads to severe emotional trauma. Adults treated in this cruel way as a child may feel slightly crazed much of the time, not sure of their sexual feelings or those of anyone who tries to become close.

I have often been asked, because I have done much research in sexual abuse of children by parents, if parents are aware of their reasons for abusing the child, particularly if the abuse is not consummated—a child is sexually teased but the sexual act is not completed. The answer to this question reveals much individual variation, even among specific groups.

Some child abusers, even if they have not consummated the sex act, retain a strong degree of awareness of their act plus deep guilt. I have treated several patients who came to me because they felt guilty about sexually immature behavior with their children. They were similar to alcoholics, who cannot control their addiction and feel ashamed and guilty. But like all human beings who find it difficult to take responsibility for the acts that hurt them and others, they tend to rationalize or repress their behavior. Many sex abusers describe their overt abuse as an act of love rather than as a selfish violation of the child's body and mind. They "justify" their behavior, much as the average person tries to rationalize inappropriate feelings or actions.

When a child is teased sexually, this creates much more disruption of psychic equilibrium than either open rejection or open seduction, I believe. In an article, "Effects of Childhood Sexual Abuse on the Psychosocial Functioning of Adults," published in *Social Work*, the Journal of the National Association of Social Workers (September/October 1988), I point out that I have treated at least fifteen men and women who were victims of open incest. Not one of them became psychotic. I have also treated children and adults abandoned by their parents and, while they suffered greatly, none of them became psychotic either.

On the other hand, I have treated many children and adults during my close to four decades of practice who were victims of excessive teasing, such as Nancy experienced. Parents paraded in the nude, regularly examined and touched the child's naked body, gave the child baths until adolescence, appeared to promise sexual gratification. The child became aroused, angry and, in some instances, was later diagnosed as schizophrenic.

Seduction to some degree exists in all relationships and most certainly in the parent-child relationship. In moderate degree it prepares the child for adult love. Seduction takes place in other rooms besides the bedroom. Parents may examine the child's bowel movements in the bathroom in a seductive way, praise the child for "producing," bribe him to produce further. They may bathe the child, massage him in a seductive manner, they may admire the child's sexual organs, looks, clothes and achievements in a flirtatious way. Excessive stimulation and abrupt frustration, which we call "teasing," may drive children and adults to madness.

It is as if they are being fed and weaned at the same time, turned on and turned off simultaneously, caressed and slapped concomitantly. This may lead to psychosis. The human organism cannot cope comfortably with emotional signals that are overwhelming and confusing.

Analysts and other helping professionals are often asked about the "genetic" or constitutional causes of schizophrenia.

Several researchers during the past decades have claimed there are certain "genes" in families that may be prime etiological factors in the cause of schizophrenia.

This research has caused many professionals and non-professionals to question whether sexual "teasing" and scapegoating induce severe psychotic reactions. I believe all of us have constitutional vulnerabilities. Just as there are constitutional propensities toward hyperactivity or extreme passivity, it is possible that, given the same stress, a person with one genetic predisposition will react in one way while a second will react differently.

In my work with schizophrenic children and adults, I have never seen one who was the recipient of tender love and care during the first years of life. Nor have I seen one schizophrenic child who lived in a family atmosphere where the mother and father loved each other. Instead, there was obvious hatred in the home of the schizophrenic—perhaps unexpressed but reflected in facial gestures, attitudes, negativism. Or, more often, openly expressed in hostility between parent and parent, and parent and child.

My experience with schizophrenic patients has consistently shown that the psychotic patient as a child has been scapegoated, stimulated and frustrated, in equal doses, and treated without sensitivity or true caring by parents.

It was obvious in Nancy's case that her brother, who had a similar genetic endowment, was experienced by both parents much less ambivalently than she was. Throughout childhood and adolescence, he never showed a sign of schizophrenic behavior. His life from cradle through mature adulthood was much freer of conflicts because his father was more consistent with him, did not "tease" him sexually. Further-more, I had the impression that his mother welcomed him more tenderly into her life than she did her daughter.

In many families of schizophrenic youngsters the child has been in some way the focus of deep parental ambivalence, as well as the recipient of mixed feelings. He may be wanted desperately at times, not wanted at others. The child consistently wished out of the way (dead and gone) is openly not wanted. It is often the inconsistency of the parent's shifting feelings that confuse the child, he is loved one moment, vilified the next.

Nancy was rarely free of conflict, often felt out of her wits. Her whole life seemed filled with suffering in one form or another. She continued to beg me to sleep with her and turned verbally violent when I refused. It was as though she screamed to the world, This is my pain, I cannot stand feeling thwarted after so many broken promises. I thought, Never, never underestimate the lasting power of the unfulfilled sexual drive.

Then, all of a sudden, in December 1981, Nancy seemed relatively free of conflict, after she released more resentment toward me. This was followed by a period of greater rapport with her husband.

She reported, "I resent sex with Paul less these days. We're also talking more kindly about each other. There's more sharing."

At times Paul, in her fantasy, represented her father and her brother, I thought. I could understand how he might sometimes find Nancy difficult to live with. Undoubtedly he possessed deep problems of his own. Nancy also mentioned she felt less irritated with her daughter Sheila and more kindly disposed toward the children at school, her colleagues and the once-despised principal.

Usually in psychoanalysis after the patient has discharged many emotions, particularly anger toward the therapist, he likes other people more. The therapist represents parts of the parents, siblings and others, thus when the patient emotes with sound and fury but the therapist does not retaliate, the patient acts less like a guilt-ridden child, more like a loved and understood youngster. He then loves and understands himself more, loses his need to battle others so violently.

As 1982 got under way, Nancy started once again arriving late for appointments. She also showed less interest in the analysis and me. Though she could be emotive and spontaneous, she now became withdrawn.

I was not really sure what caused her withdrawal until she reported a dream: "The man in it was handicapped physically." She described him as resembling Herman Stein, one of her colleagues at school. I noted his initials were the same as mine.

I said, "Apparently, you see me handicapped physically, much as you see Herman Stein."

She responded, "I don't know why I would dream of you or Herman as handicapped physically, since neither of you is."

I said, "Maybe you'd like to see us handicapped." A wish, or several wishes, always underlies a dream.

She announced sullenly, "You're always accusing me of evil motives. What do you have against me? You keep putting me down. I think you're out to weaken me."

Though I felt Nancy was projecting onto me her wishes to weaken *me*, making me the hostile perpetrator, I wanted to help her reach this insight by herself. Otherwise she would feel I was quarreling with her, not helping her.

I asked, "What do you suppose I hold against you that I would wish to 'put you down'?"

She said, "I think, like Herman Stein, you resent my competence and my intelligence. You're threatened because you are really quite weak."

The more she discussed my weakness, my limitations, my envy, yet realized I could listen patiently to her putdowns, she slowly began to talk of her own envy, her feelings of being weak.

She reached this stage after telling me in one session how smug I appeared when she said she was feeling better as a result of the therapy. That was indeed quite an admission from her. She promptly undid it.

She sneered. "You think you're a big prick when you make me feel better, don't you? You seem so in love with yourself." Then angrily: "I'd like to kick you in the balls and yank off that big prick of yours."

I said, "Then I'd be handicapped physically, like you pictured me in your dream."

Nancy did not welcome this interpretation. It is difficult at first for many patients to understand dream symbolism, especially sexual and violent symbolism. She snapped,

"There you go again, waving your brilliance in the air. You're just like my exhibitionistic father who thought he knew it all."

I waited for her to continue, thinking, For a woman who writes quite brilliant poetry at times, she can speak like a longshoreman when she hits the couch. I wonder which side will emerge next?

When I reflected on the frequent duality of Nancy's speech, I understood why the schizophrenic is often called a "split personality." While many of us play a number of roles in various settings, there tends to be a "self" that is reasonably consistent. A man's behavior in his office will be similar in many ways to his behavior with his spouse, friends, neighbors. Differences exist within the mature personality, yet he possesses a higher degree of what therapists call an "integrated self."

But the schizophrenic patient does more than enact different roles. He assumes various identities as Sybil did in the book bearing her name by the late Flora Rheta Schreiber. The schizophrenic has to assume different selves because he is convinced he will be annihilated for what he does or thinks. Nancy yearned to be a poet but, when feeling poetic, her sexual wishes were stirred. As they reached consciousness, she then expected punishment and turned into the antithesis of a poet—a cold, calculating attorney like her image of her brother.

Yet when she felt like an attorney—a man like her father or brother—she became terror-stricken of that identity too (unconsciously she wished to steal their penis and be as powerful as they were). She either reverted again to a poet or, more often, as seen in my office, a helpless, whining little girl.

Following my interpretation of Nancy's wishing to "yank off" my penis, after a long silence she said with a sigh, "If my father had it all, why didn't he give it to me?" Then: "When I teach grammar I often think of a dangling participle. I guess because my father always dangled seduction in front of me." She added, "You do the same."

Her wish to castrate me and her wish to castrate her father were followed by dreams in which she actively played the role of a boy. She recalled memories when she competed at eight and nine with boys both on the basketball court and in the classroom. I believed her mother had wished her first-born to be a boy, perhaps also her father. Nancy responded consciously and unconsciously to their unspoken wishes which she sensed, feeling she had to fulfill them in some way. Such a wish is often conveyed to the little girl as she grows up, intensifying her wishes to be a boy, which, she feels, would give her more sexual pleasure, less pain and more power in life.

Nancy admitted, as though confiding a carefully guarded secret, "When I felt so alone growing up without a mother, and a father who was so up and down I could never tell what he felt, I tried to be self-sufficient. Many times I wanted to be a wonderwoman or a tomboy so I wouldn't have to depend on anybody."

The little princess who wished to be a tomboy or wonderwoman so her parents would love her better, I thought.

Neither role could possibly bring her happiness, allow her to esteem herself as girl or woman.

At the end of February 1982, Nancy again threatened to abandon treatment. She seemed to wish to be more self-sufficient, not depend on me. She spent several sessions demeaning psychoanalysis, Freud and some of my articles in the journal with which she became familiar. I thought the best thing at this time was to listen carefully with limited interruption, otherwise she would fight all the harder.

I became somewhat worried though, when once again she seemed paranoid. In one session she exclaimed, "I can tell the way you greet me that you really want to get rid of me. Sometimes I feel you're going to rise from your chair and suddenly hit me when I accuse you of having limitations."

Several times she asked, "Why do you hate me so? I know you do, don't deny it."

I told her, "When you hate me, you're very worried I will retaliate. You still do not believe I am here to help you, to understand you."

She said a bit wistfully, in a tone I had not heard for weeks, "I wish you would get angry and not be here just to understand me. Why can't I get a rise out of you?"

"If I get angry and you get a rise out of me, it will be like having sex, won't it?"

She responded, "And that's the last thing in the world you want to do, you stupid moron, isn't it? You stimulate and tease but you never come through. Just like my father."

Then, in quieter voice, "At times I feel I'm about to become your woman. And then once again you let me down, just what my father did. I thought I was his princess but he abandoned me.

"I think any girl who is promised a lot by her father but gets only a fraction of what she desires, wants to kick him in the balls and take away his cock." She added, "Maybe keep it for herself."

This theme would come up often in Nancy's analysis and, perhaps, is the best explanation of why girls want to be boys. When a girl wants her father sexually and cannot have him, she tries to *be* her father, "self-sufficient and strong," as Nancy experienced her father.

The same is true when boys want to be girls or women. If they wish their mother sexually with more than average intensity (encouraged by the mother to do so) and cannot have her, they try to become a mother to themselves. I learned repeatedly from Nancy that often the roots of bisexuality, homosexuality and multiple personality lie in the fact that we try to become, often do become, what we cannot have but desperately wish to possess.

The more I worked with Nancy, the more I understood the desperation and terror of someone who was intensely demanding, enormously clinging and frequently hostile. These characteristics never make a person likable and the analyst, like everyone else, often feels irritated when a "Nancy" tries to manipulate, coerce and demean.

But the analyst must go several steps beyond irritation. He understands the demanding baby in himself, recognizes also his envy of an adult who feels free to express what the analyst must repress. The most difficult part of my work with Nancy was to acknowledge constantly the "Nancy" in me who "wants what I want when I want it" but cannot have it and feels angry.

I believe severed souls like Nancy upset most of us because they express what we feel we must control. The schizophrenic patient is dealt with so punitively by mental health professionals because he stirs in them the infantile yearnings they dare not gratify.

When a schizophrenic patient demands gratification immediately, many professionals, like those in Nancy's life, respond, in effect, "How dare you demand to be a gratified infant? I can't get what you want, therefore I'll punish you for wanting it. You express the very thing I cannot bear to think about." This is tantamount to saying to the emotionally ill patient, "Goddamn you! You can go to hell." They are already in hell, the "hell" of their tormenting, buried childhood fantasies, fears and guilts.

Nancy would have to face and understand her furies before she could feel more like a tender, loving woman, before she could accept herself as a warm, compassionate human being who could be more fully wife and mother.

P   A   R

T III

THE
THIRD
YEAR

SPRING
1982

7

GROWING
UP TOO
SWIFTLY

**April to July
1982**

Psychoanalysts have learned that to be effective with the patient, the analyst must be able to step into the patient's psychic shoes, so to speak. He has to feel within himself the patient's emotions, fantasies and conflicts.

The more the analyst can identify with the patient and say to himself, "I have been here too," the more he can truly empathize with and help the patient recover. These were the kind of thoughts that predominated as I began my third year of analysis with Nancy.

If the analyst does not identify with the patient's problems, he will unconsciously try to dismiss their essential meaning and be unable to help the patient resolve his misery.

One of the main reasons most therapists have not felt comfortable with schizophrenic patients is because they have not acknowledged their own natural proclivities toward psychosis. Since the days of Freud they have in essence (albeit unconsciously) said to the schizophrenic patient, "You remind me of my own craziness. You infuriate me when I see your irrationalities, for then I am forced to face my own. If I do not have to see you frequently, I do not have to examine my own craziness too often. If I maintain only a superficial relationship with you, I'll maintain only a superficial relationship with my own craziness." Most therapists do not face their negative feelings toward schizophrenic patients because they do not want to realize how intolerant they are of their own childishness and primitive urges.

Most analysts have tried to justify their hostility toward schizophrenic patients by offering theoretical concepts to explain the causes of the "disease." Freud himself described schizophrenia as a "narcissistic neurosis." He pointed out that because the patient was so self-involved, he could not form a "therapeutic alliance" with the analyst and hence was essentially untreatable.

In 1928, Freud told the Hungarian psychoanalyst Istvan Hollos that he resisted dealing with psychotics. Freud explained, "Finally, I confessed to myself that I do not like

these sick people, that I am angry at them because I feel
them so far from me and all that is human."

Freud stated he had never known a patient "the germs
of whose disease" he had not seen in himself. But when it
came to psychosis, Freud could not practice what he himself
advocated. In facing his personal reactions toward schizophrenic patients, Freud was indeed candid in acknowledging
his dislike of treating them. The eminent genius and compassionate humanitarian viewed schizophrenics as distant
from himself and "far from all that is human."

Psychiatry's fear of psychotherapy with schizophrenics
was recently shown after psychiatrist Dr. Peter Breggin appeared on "The Oprah Winfrey Show." He enumerated the
serious medical problems that follow shock treatment or the
use of drugs. He cited evidence that such treatments can
cause permanent neurological damage and other serious physical and emotional problems.

One of the most prominent authorities on the psychoth-
erapeutic treatment of schizophrenics is the Michigan psychologist and psychoanalyst, Dr. Bertram Karon. He has
achieved widespread success in analytic treatment of schizophrenic patients. Dr. Karon's research not only reveals that
the schizophrenic patient is a product essentially of poor
nurturing and poor interpersonal relationships in childhood,
but also suggests that when the therapist conceives of himself
as similar to the patient, therapy proves quite successful.
Both his research and humane perspectives have been so
outstanding that he was recently awarded the title "Distin-
guished Psychoanalyst of the Year" by the New York Society
for Psychoanalytic Training.

Dr. Karon has carried out extensive research on and treatment of the schizophrenic patient. He refers to psychotherapy of the schizophrenic patient as the "treatment of choice." Through rigorous research he has shown that even a small amount of psychotherapy for the schizophrenic patient is both "more effective and less costly" than medication. He also believes that because the schizophrenic patient has been deeply injured emotionally by human relationships, he needs a "corrective human relationship" that is consistent, rather than ambivalent. One that is humane rather than punitive, caring rather than indifferent or hateful.

My interest in psychosis emerges from the story of my own life. In my book, *Behind the Couch*, I described taking my comprehensive examinations for a doctorate at Columbia University. During the oral part of the examination the professor asked me to explain and describe diagnostic labels such as "hebephrenic," "schizophrenic," "paranoid schizophrenic," "borderline personality" and "manic-depressive psychosis."

When the examination was over, the professor averred, "I assume you were thinking of real patients when you answered my questions with so much fervor." Then he asked, "Are they in treatment now?"

I laughed, then told him the truth. "Each label you gave me described a relative I knew well. I've had years of experience with all of them."

One of the major reasons I have felt reasonably comfortable with schizophrenics is because I had to learn to cope with seriously disturbed relatives throughout childhood and adolescence. I witnessed paranoid thinking at the dinner ta-

ble. I saw manic-depressive psychosis and hebephrenic schizophrenia at family get-togethers. Furthermore, I became
sensitized rather early in life to my own primitive wishes and
bizarre fantasies.

One major drive I shared with Nancy was a powerful
urge to produce. Both of us, for different reasons, felt a strong
obligation to act adult during childhood. Both felt pressured,
then resentful. Both found it difficult to know what to do with
the hatred we felt, most of which we consigned to unaware-
ness.

I was not very acceptable to my parents and extended
family if I did not come first in my class, if I did not hit home
runs and if I did not beat out any youngster who competed
with me in any way. While I spent many hours in my own
personal analysis dealing with these issues and felt much
more at peace with myself by the time I met Nancy, nonetheless I could genuinely identify with the pressures she felt
as a child and adolescent—pressures that caused much rage.

During spring 1982 Nancy started to focus on the fact
that she could not like herself unless she was an achiever.
One day she came to a session, threw herself on the couch
and announced, "I've had another argument with the principal. The son-of-a-bitch never appreciates me, no matter
what I do. My pupils put on marvelous plays, everyone of
them does a superb job of acting and what does that con-
descending shithead say? 'Not bad.' That's all he says, 'Not
bad.'"

I kept quiet, wanting more of her thoughts. She turned

on me, as I anticipated, said, "You don't appreciate me, either. I suppose, Strean, you're also thinking, 'Not bad.' "

Then she sneered, "You give me credit for nothing. As a matter of fact, I pay you promptly at the end of each month but you won't even give me credit for that."

Silence, then "I feel all I do here is produce and produce and produce. You never praise me. You never reward me. All you do is ask me to give you more dreams, more fantasies and more 'psychoanalyeze' to indulge yourself."

While many patients made similar accusations—every patient wants the analyst to be the perfect parent who loves him constantly and consistently—Nancy's complaints were harsher and more intense. All patients resent their parents' failure to give them full attention every minute of the day, and all patients can point to times in their lives when parents were unavailable physically and emotionally.

At this stage of treatment I had to offer Nancy the opportunity to vent her anger at me, as I appeared like a difficult taskmaster. Thus I kept silent for a number of sessions as she castigated me for demanding much and giving little, criticized her mother and father for the same behavior.

Then, one day with a certain realistic appraisal of me, Nancy said, "I'll bet you take notes on my sessions for your books. You're more interested in fame and fortune than helping me."

As I remained quiet, she tried to force me into an argument by saying once again, "You have no defense, have you? You're a selfish, narcissistic bastard. Sometimes I think you're like my brother who always wanted to surpass me and who got all the praise because he was a boy."

While Nancy hurled invectives, she also now brought forth the many unshed tears held back during childhood and adolescence. She cried for long periods, far more than the average patient. She had deeper hurts to cry about, I thought.

Drying her tears during one session, she said sadly, "Who was I to go to when my mother lay sick and dying, my brother did nothing but tease me and my father was busy with patients? I'd head for my room and lie on the bed like a corpse."

Identifying with her dying mother, I thought. She went on, "Sometimes I felt I was drowning"—submerged in tears.

I suggested, and only had to suggest it once, "Drowning is something you've been very afraid of. You're terrified of the many tears inside you, tears you have never shed."

This gave Nancy permission to feel free to sob away many an analytic hour. She pointed out that when she was confined to mental hospitals, as she would cry in front of a psychiatrist he would respond, "Now, control yourself!"

"Once when I tried to cry and the doctor wouldn't let me, I developed an acute migraine headache," she recalled. "When I told him I had a splitting headache, he accused me of being a malingerer. I said he didn't understand me and he put me in seclusion."

What Nancy reported illustrates what happens to thousands of schizophrenic patients. They are not permitted to bring up the thoughts that lie "too deep for tears."

I became convinced at this point in Nancy's treatment how crucial it is to help the schizophrenic patient say whatever is on his mind. Nancy verified this one day in May 1982 when she said, "The big difference between you and my previous doctors is that you let me cry and scream. You never seem frightened of my craziness."

During her treatment she must have said, at least a hundred times, "You never seem frightened of my craziness."

As she cried and discharged her verbal resentment, she began to feel the start of an inner peace she had never known. One day she said thoughtfully, "If only someone had let me cry when my mother was sick and dying, or let me express anger when I felt so neglected. Then I wouldn't have needed to be carted away to mental hospitals."

Although she both felt and functioned better, loud voices from the past still persisted and conflicts remained far from resolved. A week or two after she told me she felt the freest she had in years, Nancy arrived at a session in late May as depressed as I had ever seen her.

She lamented, "I'm not sleeping. I'm not eating. I've thought several times of cutting myself with a razor."

There was a desperation in her voice that sounded powerful and a dependency that seemed profound. She went on, "I was feeling pretty good for a while, but now I'm reminded of how I felt in the mental hospitals. A few times lately I've heard voices saying, 'Nancy, you're a bad girl. Nancy, you don't deserve to live.' "

She then started to berate me, although she fused her criticisms with apologies. She said, "It's hard for me to tell you this but the therapy isn't working. I'm not angry at you for not being able to help me because I know you've tried your best."

It is not unusual for a patient to make progress, feel better, only to become miserable and unhappy after enjoying the elation that accompanies therapeutic progress. The founder of psychoanalysis discovered this phenomenon, called it the "negative therapeutic reaction." Freud pointed out that when patients are guilt-ridden and possess a punitive conscience, or what analysts call "a punishing superego," they cannot permit themselves to enjoy much pleasure. Pleasure is experienced as defying parents or antagonizing the "voices" of parents and other authorities who speak out in the patient's conscience or superego. For this defiance the patient must punish himself, as he was punished when a child.

The healthy, mature person and the one who has reaped the benefits of therapy both are able to enjoy pleasure without punishment. They can accept pleasure without self-recrimination because they have given up the fantasied battles of childhood.

Many children, perhaps most, grow up with the notion that sex is "bad" and "forbidden," and therefore become convinced sexual pleasure should be repressed and suppressed. But most, if not all children still wish to gratify their sexual desires. "If mother and father are against sex," the child reasons, "then I have to defy them."

The child then embarks on a fantasied battle with his parents each time he imagines sexual intimacy or "plays doctor" with a member of the opposite sex. It is the defiant, angry feeling toward parents that makes the child guilty, after which he suffers depression, almost always an accompaniment of guilt. He then unconsciously seeks punishment because of the guilt.

Analysts have also learned that patients who respond with a "negative therapeutic reaction," as children have fought intense battles with their parents. Later, they reca-pitulate the battle with their analysts. To resolve the depres-sion and diminish the guilt that are the major components of the negative therapeutic reaction, the analyst must help a patient understand the battle he wages with his parents, which duplicates and precedes the one with the analyst. Then he can make peace with the parental voices with whom he has been at war. This enables him eventually to enjoy and sustain pleasure in work and love.

To help Nancy make peace with her inner parental voices would not be an easy task. I had experienced negative therapeutic reactions with virtually every patient I treated, of all ages. Each patient needed to punish himself after feeling he had defied a parent. But Nancy's depression was far more intense than that of most patients.

It is one thing for a patient to say, "I feel depressed, I feel sad, I'm not up to snuff, I am lonely." This is par for the psychic course. But Nancy talked of not eating and sleep-ing, of feeling suicidal, and heard voices that held delusions of persecution—a phenomenon that suggests the onset of psychosis.

All of us at times hear the voices of our parents but most of us recognize these voices are reactivated memories and fantasies that are self-created, much as we recognize that a dream is something we ourselves have scripted. But when someone believes the voices are actually in the room talking to him and has no awareness that he is creating them, this indicates psychosis.

One of the difficult lessons I learned as a psychoanalyst was to empathize with psychotic behavior and respond to it as something the patient was "really" experiencing in the here and now. It is tempting to tell a patient suffering persecution delusions, "You've done nothing wrong and there are no voices in the room." When I almost did this early in my career with psychotic children and adults, inevitably these patients felt misunderstood, isolated themselves from me and considered me still another enemy in their lives, although at times a friendly one.

Any astute attendant in a mental hospital knows that to persuade a patient who thinks he is Julius Caesar to make his bed, he has to say, "Caesar, please make your bed." If he says, "Mr. Smith, please make your bed," the patient usually balks.

Thus when Nancy told me she heard voices saying she was a bad girl, I asked, "What have you been doing that you believe is bad?"

I expected her to tell me that in one way or another she was defying her parents in fantasy, but her response both surprised and intrigued me.

After a moment or two of silence, she said slowly, "I am a bad girl because I'm in therapy with you!"

Initially this was the last thing I thought she would say but as I listened carefully, she made perfect sense. She taught me a great deal more about the "negative therapeutic reaction."

I asked, "What is wrong about being in therapy with me?"

She spent the better part of several sessions giving me a most comprehensive and illuminating answer. She started with, "If my mother or father knew I was here on the couch, they'd violently disapprove and angrily reject me. To seek your understanding and help would be a crime to them. I am supposed to get only *their* understanding and help."

She fell quiet for a few moments, then went on, "When I'm with you I feel like a child who has run away from home and is having a ball with a foster parent. In many ways, when I'm here, particularly when I think you're helping me, I feel like a child who has wiped out his parents and lives in the Garden of Eden. I am a traitor."

One of the questions I had to answer for myself, and eventually help Nancy answer for herself, was how did she become so sadistic? Like all sadistic persons, Nancy as a child and growing girl was exposed to deep humiliations, teasing and demeaning remarks and behavior by her father and brother. And like everyone who becomes sadistic, she felt weak and vulnerable compared to those who appeared strong and in charge. The masochistic child becomes the sadistic adult, copying those who have persecuted him.

The emphatic and disciplined analyst reminds himself constantly, as I had to do with Nancy, that whenever sadism is present in the patient, the latter feels weak and vulnerable. He tries as hard as he can to appear strong, the one in power. We might describe a sadist as a frightened child arming himself with guns and bows and arrows so he does not have to recapture the pain of his terrorizing childhood.

Nancy seemed to be saying, "I've never realized why pleasure of any kind is so disturbing to me. Every time I'm with somebody who treats me nicely I turn on them as if I'm telling my parents to drop dead."

Then she told me she now understood why, when her

relationship with her husband and daughter was going well, she had to undo it. She seemed more in touch with a voice of her own that said, "I'm having a better relationship with my husband than you two, as my parents, did. And a better relationship with my daughter than you had with me."

She had feared her parents would get even with her for living more happily than they did, a fear many of us share. But Nancy, like all emotionally disturbed patients, felt it more so.

She conveyed a more important message than any of the best-selling self-help books. She clearly and eloquently pointed out that if you want to be "your own best friend" or wish to "let go of guilt" or "take charge of your life" or "win friends and influence people" or possess "peace of mind," the main way to do so is to tame your wish for vengeance, your hatred and murderous feelings in childhood toward the parents. Those who cannot enjoy success in work and/or love still put their energy into fighting past battles.

Nancy was starting to get in touch with her intense battle with her mother and father and their current representatives—her school principal, her colleagues, her husband, her analyst and others. She realized that each time she experienced pleasure she became involved in a battle that never proved productive or enhanced her in any way. Realizing this futility diminished her depression, helped her start to build her self-esteem. By the middle of June she felt more buoyant, more content at work and at home.

This progress occurred not so much as a conscious decision but a lessening of her fight with her parents (the parts of them she had internalized, as all children do to some degree). This also lessened her need to punish herself. Analysts know that the depressed, guilt-ridden patient needs the chance to come to grips with what he punishes himself for—usually his murderous feelings and fantasies. As Nancy could express her wish to kill her mother and father and realized I did not want to punish her for this, she became more self-accepting, less guilty and less depressed.

But, as is always true in analysis, there is no rest for the analyst and the patient. No sooner did she tell me her life was improving, her depression diminishing, her suicidal thoughts disappearing, than Nancy once again lost enthusiasm for life and therapy.

She did not, however, become as depressed as before, but started subtly to demean her therapy and to demean me yet again. She sounded whiny, irritable and impatient.

It is this kind of reaction from patients that causes psychoanalysts to refer at times to their work as the "impossible profession," Freud's description. It certainly is not the easiest task in the world to help a suicidal, depressed, guilt-ridden, delusional woman start to overcome her problems only to find yourself demeaned, derogated and denounced.

I thought at this time of my own mother whom I experienced as never satisfied with me. If I cleaned my room, she berated me for not doing homework. If I did my homework, she thought I should be learning to become more courteous. I had to be careful several times not to make Nancy my taskmaster mother. Whenever I felt resentment toward Nancy,

I knew I was unconsciously looking at her as a punitive mother instead of a desperate patient.

At first I wondered if Nancy's now coming late for sessions, showing limited enthusiasm for me and for her therapy, had something to do with the upcoming summer vacation. I could not be sure, and whenever I am not sure what is happening with a patient, I work overtime to be quiet and listen to free associations, dreams and particularly transference fantasies.

In this situation I am very influenced by a sign Freud was reputed to have placed on his desk: "When in doubt, don't."

All I knew for certain was that Nancy arrived late for sessions and showed a lack of energy and interest in her analysis. Toward the start of July I said, "You've been coming late recently and don't seem to have much interest in our work. What do you suppose this is all about?"

She asked somewhat belligerently, "You're always so curious about what goes on in me. What makes you so curious?"

"You sound irritated," I said.

She replied, "You sound like a pompous ass."

I said not a word. She went on, "You enjoy your work too much. You're a professional voyeur and a psychopathic psychological surgeon. You are too damned smug and arrogant."

She next said (and it stung), "I think you do this work

so you can write books and get glory out of what you do for a living. It inflates your ego."

She had seized on something true enough about me. But I had to keep in mind, as she berated me, that no matter how much I was a "narcissistic bore," Nancy was indulging in a tirade and wanted to knock me down with acid words.

Most patients, when feeling a negative transference — hate for the analyst—usually pick on some part of the analyst that is quite real. If the analyst feels too defensive about such criticism, he cannot see beyond himself to the best interests of the patient.

At this point in our relationship, Nancy was clearly observing the satisfaction I felt from helping her and the pleasure I derived from writing. By now she had read several of my books and sensed my enthusiasm for work. But she was also using what she learned about me for attack. This I had to interpret to her.

At other times she would use my enthusiasm for writing to praise me when she was in a positive transference. But at this juncture there was no praise. I said to her, "You resent me very much these days. Particularly, you resent the pleasure I derive from my work. I get the impression you don't want me to enjoy myself."

Nancy said, almost enthusiastically, "You're damned right. I hate the fact that you use me and exploit me to enhance your professional reputation. You remind me of my father who did the same thing. He used his patients and me to make himself a big prick."

Then she recalled, "Last night I dreamed that my father was a psychoanalyst. I was lying on the couch and could not see him but I could hear him breathing very hard—so hard that I turned around to see what was going on. He had a big erection and I yelled out, 'You're trying to give me a royal screwing.' Then I got up and went over to where he sat and punched him in the balls and said, 'You big prick!' "

Although I found this dream interesting, I kept quiet for two reasons. Anything I might say would only further Nancy's notion that I was "a big prick," using her to enhance my own sexual and professional interests. But also Nancy was quite capable of associating to her own dreams by now. As is true with virtually all patients as they become convinced dreams have a specific meaning in their lives. They are then able to free-associate on their own to the various parts of the dream, make their own interpretations. Slowly they become their own analysts as they prepare to continue the work by themselves after they leave the couch permanently.

When Nancy realized I was not going to react to her vivid dream, she began telling me her thoughts about it. She said, "I guess I see you and my father as one and the same person. And I guess I see you as getting very turned on by my lying on the couch and talking to you. It's similar to my lying down as a little girl when my father examined my body if anything hurt. Sometimes he would hurt me more as he explored. That's how I feel about you at times."

She fell silent a moment, then went on, "And both of you are out to exploit me, to use me to get a hard-on. You make me so angry I want to castrate you." Her tone sounded furious.

She spoke only half the truth. Since it was her dream, she had the wish to make both her father and me sexually excited. Then, on noting he or I became aroused, she would want to hurt us.

I asked, "Why do you suppose you get so angry after you turn me on?"

She laughed and it was a hearty laugh. I was unsure what her laughter meant but she soon told me.

She admitted, "I never knew I had the capacity to turn you on and that makes me feel quite gleeful and powerful. When I notice that you or any man responds to me, at first I feel good. But then something deep inside takes over and I hate you."

I asked, "When you see me in the dream or imagine your father, or husband, or any man with a hard-on, what makes you feel so angry?"

The words were hardly out of my mouth when she berated me with intense anger. "There you go again, you no-good Freudian bastard! You're trying to get me to say I suffer from penis envy. You *are* a motherfucker. You try to confirm your theories, seduce me, get me to turn you on only so I will admire that goddamn thing between your legs. That—that—"—then the words exploded—"dangling participle."

I knew that in addition to her general anger at men, the approaching vacation disturbed her. It was a separation she feared and hated. So I sat back, kept quiet. She needed me to say little so she could say a lot. There was now much on her active mind.

She described in the next several sessions how she experienced men and their sexuality. "I always felt that the man was so much more powerful than the woman. My father lived, my mother died. I was scapegoated, my brother was loved and admired."

Then in a low, wistful voice: "I remember even at five and six wanting so much to be a boy. I would stand at the toilet and try to pee like a boy. Later, I tried to pretend my clitoris was a cock. As I rubbed it, I often imagined I was a man either jerking off or screwing a woman."

Nancy recalled other instances of wishing to be a boy or man—men and boys have fantasies of being girls and women while girls and women fantasy being boys and men. It was important for her not to just talk about her envy and desire to be a boy but to put into words what she repudiated in a woman.

I said to Nancy, "There must be something about your vagina you don't like."

She gave many immediate thoughts. "Yes, you're right. It's like a garbage can, a wastepaper basket, a toilet bowl. A place where men can put their dicks and have their fun but where there isn't much pleasure for me."

As Nancy recalled how much she loathed her vagina, several times referring to it as "an open wound," I remembered the dream where she wanted to remove my penis. Patients frequently wish to do to others what they feel has been done unto them to cause pain.

I put together her wish to castrate me, as well as the fantasy of her vagina as an open wound, and made an interpretation. "There was a time when you were a little girl and believed you too, like a boy, had a penis. You felt for some reason it was ripped off and you've been suffering from an open wound ever since."

She asked, as though she had been searching for the answer, "Is that why all the blood comes out every month?"

"Is this what you have believed all these years?"

I reminded myself this was a common fantasy in women—the shedding of monthly blood, necessary for producing a baby, was often imagined as the result of castration. I recalled one little girl patient who asked, "Why should a boy have something I don't have? That isn't fair, is it?"

Nancy spent the next few sessions validating the fantasy she had been castrated as a little girl. It took many forms. Her mother did not really want a girl but a boy, so Nancy grew a penis, then it was cut off by her mother during an argument. She grew it again and her father, during another argument, ripped it off. It also was taken from her at times she was a "bad" girl, when she hated her mother, father and brother. She admitted she had spent much time during her childhood imagining she once had a penis only to have it removed. At times this fantasy became obsessive, controlling her for weeks occasionally.

She recalled how at school she competed with boys academically, often equating her brain with a penis. She played tennis with boys, relished the notion of having "balls of my own" that gave her courage and the drive to be the athletic equal of any boy.

While Nancy's memories and fantasies at this time surfaced quite spontaneously, they had to be interrupted by the prospect of my August vacation. As is true with most patients, she again experienced the separation with great resentment.

She told me, "If I were a man, you'd want to stay here and work with me. You'd get interesting material and great insights. But I'm just a lousy woman—girl—with an open wound, so why would you want to favor me?"

She described more examples of her parents' favoring her brother. I was able to make an interpretation that helped her considerably.

I said, "If you were a male patient, like your brother, I would grant all your desires, you believe. You think that if only you were a boy, you could live in the Garden of Eden, where all your wishes would be granted."

Slowly she started to accept that she had felt ever since the birth of her brother that boys were all-powerful while she, as a girl, was doomed to suffer because of her inferiority— the lack of the magical penis. As she could admit this, she moved toward more acceptance of herself as a woman.

In her last session before vacation, she said poignantly, "Even your men patients aren't going to have you during August. Nobody has everything. Not even men."

This was quite different from the Nancy of previous summers when she became furious, wanted at first to take her own life. This showed me and, I believe, showed her, she was coming closer to accepting what all successfully analyzed patients must accept—*reality as it is*, which means understanding and eventually giving up your infantile feelings of grandiosity. This is a difficult task for most of us.

8
WHO'S GOT
THE
POWER?

**Fall and Winter
1982–83**

As I drove my red Toyota across the George Washington Bridge from my home in New Jersey, the early-morning sun streamed down, warming my face. The soft breeze from the Hudson River felt exhilarating.

It was my first day back to work after a summer vacation of four weeks. I thought of how the past month had become so meaningful a time for both patient and analyst, enough for Judith Rossner to write a novel on the subject, aptly titled *August.*

While there has been a lot of psychoanalytic literature on what transpires in the patient's life when the analyst vacates his office to relax, there is little mention of what happens to the analyst. I recall just after my book *Behind the Couch* appeared in spring 1988, many readers and TV and radio interviewers asked me, "How come you did not speak of what you feel and what you do during August?"

When I vacation in the Adirondacks, I constantly am aware I do not watch the clock. One of the major activities of an analyst is clock-watching, during August I notice my neck feels more relaxed because I am not craning it constantly in the direction of my office clock.

Whenever I contrast the freedom to come and go as I please on vacation with my set schedule during the work year, I am always reminded of the deep responsibility I feel for my patients and how, in many ways, they control my life. As I drove south along Riverside Drive to my office in September 1982, I reflected on the mixed feelings I had, and always have had, on my first day back at work.

On the one hand, there is an exhilaration as I look forward to hearing how my patients have fared and what new challenges I face. And, what is rarely mentioned by analysts about August is that I, and most of my colleagues I am sure, have missed their patients to some extent. In many ways going back to work in September is for me similar to returning home for a family reunion.

Incidentally, many question the three-, four- or five-times-a week analysis because it is so costly. There is no doubt that, like major surgery, psychoanalysis involves not only a strong emotional, but also a major financial investment. Often overlooked, however, is that many analysts have a sliding fee scale and are quite ready to adjust their fees to the patient's financial situation.

Furthermore, most psychoanalytic institutes, such as the one of which I am director, the New York Center for Psychoanalytic Training, have clinics where men and women with modest or low incomes may be helped at very reasonable fees. I believe we are currently living in a day and age when psychoanalytic therapy, even three to four days a week, is available at a fee for anyone who really desires to undertake it.

When I am away from patients for a month I truly miss them, much as I miss family members when I do not see them. Of course, for me, returning to work also has its negatives. I am back to clock-watching, to examining carefully my patients' and my own free associations. I have to cope with my patients' demands, conflicts, angers and miseries which, particularly in contrast to carefree summer days, is difficult work.

I have noted during my first few days back that when my first patient has been with me for ten minutes, I feel like I have worked for ten hours. I am often quite tired after only a few minutes in the analyst's chair. Obviously this weariness and constant clock-watching—where a minute may seem like an hour—is an expression of my wish to still be in the mountains—the child's wish that life be an eternal vacation. It tells me that a part of me resents working, would like to return to playing golf and swimming.

To concentrate on work after you have enjoyed vacation means to move from being a child to the role of adult. Adults must go through this transition many times a week. It is one of the difficult rules of the human condition that we cannot be children forever, as much as we may fight this reality.

As I turned the corner into my garage on the street in back of the building that houses my office, I thought of Nancy, wondered how she had fared during the summer of 1982. How a patient feels and functions during the summer's hiatus provides a reasonably accurate barometer of analytic progress.

The patient who regresses severely and becomes quite suicidal and depressed, as Nancy did during her first summer away from me, needs a great deal more treatment. This patient is saying to the analyst in effect, "I need to be with you in order to keep alive."

Some patients function better during the analyst's absence than over the course of the analytic year. These are the patients who, in some ways, are like defiant children. They say to the analyst, "Who needs you? I can do well without you."

Other patients function exactly the same during summer as the rest of the year. They say in essence, "You're not a very important person in my life and what you do or don't do has no effect on me."

Most patients show a mixture of all these reactions but the more free of conflict the vacation days are, the more the patient indicates progress has been made—not always, but most of the time. I say not always because there is a certain patient who functions reasonably well when the analyst is not present but when he returns, the patient becomes like a child, demands to be indulged. The stimulation of the analyst's presence activates a regression similar to that of certain adults who function quite autonomously while on their own but after a visit to parents start behaving in infantile fashion.

How did Nancy do during her third major separation from me? When I greeted her in the waiting room on the Tuesday following Labor Day, she smiled with obvious warmth. Then she said spontaneously, "It's good to see you. I missed you."

She wore a fashionable dark blue silk dress, her usual high heels. But her hair was curled in new fashion. She looked far different from the highly disturbed woman I had first met. As I listened to her words of greeting, I realized that they indicated welcome news of her progress. I felt happy to see her, I had missed her. I knew she had worked as hard as she could to try to understand more of her unknown self. I did not tell her this for it would have endangered her flow of free associations—my positive feelings might influence her to censor what was on her mind.

I felt back at work as the disciplined analyst who should not tell a patient how he feels when he greets him. To do so would contaminate the patient's spontaneous thoughts and feelings. If I were to express to Nancy or any other patient how I felt on seeing her, she would react to my response rather than feel the freedom to say exactly what came to mind.

In the few seconds of walking from the waiting room to the consultation room, I said to myself in approval, Nancy no longer appears schizophrenic. Rather, she seems like a typical analysand who is neurotic. A neurotic patient may suffer from anxiety, obsessions or compulsions, depressions or psychosomatic illnesses, problems in marriage or parent-child relationships, but is not excessively paranoid.

One of the major differences between a schizophrenic patient and a neurotic is that the latter is able to trust another human being enough so he does not worry excessively about being abandoned or destroyed. Nancy now clearly showed me that though I had been away for a month, she did not consider this a desertion. She had developed enough trust so she did not fear abandonment or destruction.

As soon as she lay on the couch, she said, "I had a pretty good summer. Paul, Sheila and I relaxed at Cape Cod for three weeks. We all seemed to enjoy each other. Sex with Paul was quite satisfying and we were comfortable together most of the time. Sheila and I felt closer and that was good too."

She added, "I thought of you many times. I imagined a warm and benign expression on your face."

Then Nancy described a dream. "This dream bears out your warmth for and approval of me. I dreamed Paul and I were getting married and you officiated at the wedding. It felt good to have your permission for a happy marriage and a lively sex life."

She went on, "This summer I was able to be thoughtful about my life at times. One of the things I remembered is that I am almost the same age my mother was when she died. I used to be afraid I would die when I reached that age. But analysis has helped me feel I am entitled to keep living."

She was silent a minute. Then continued, "I kept recalling the many times we talked about my mistaken belief

that I killed my mother. I've learned from you—one of the
many things I value—that wishes do not kill. I did not kill
my mother. I do not have to feel guilty because my mother
is dead. I can stay alive and enjoy myself with Paul and
Sheila."

I was pleased to hear her say this. It seemed genuine
progress for her to become aware she did not need to be
punished for living because her mother had died early in
life—she now realized she did not have the power to decree
her mother's death.

This proved a giant step forward in her analysis. Unfortunately, too many adults carry the childish belief they are
the cause of both the good and the bad in their own lives and
the lives of their mother and father, live under its fearful
impact.

Although Nancy had achieved progress in realizing this
fantasy was not true, I reminded myself as I listened to her
enthusiastic reports of the summer and her positive feelings
toward her husband, daughter and me, that learning, in
psychoanalysis is never a linear path. While I was tempted
to join Nancy in her enthusiasm, I knew the best test of her
progress would be to see how long she could sustain positive
feelings about her marriage, her relationship with her daughter, her job and her therapist.

We were only into the third week of September when it
became clear that much analytic work remained ahead. One
day Nancy revealed a dream in which the principal of the
school told her she had done a good teaching job. On hearing

this, she slapped his face. He was a "chauvinistic male pig," she said, "who demeans the staff and always acts in a haughty, superior manner. He often goes to the board of education to take credit for all the work the staff does while we get lost in the shuffle."

I knew unconsciously she was also talking about her resentment toward me. I was the one trying to "take credit" for all her analytic progress and she felt "lost in the shuffle."

Although it was quite clear her anger toward the principal was a displacement of her anger for me, I did not want to interpret this to her at the moment. Then I would appear to her as the "big shot who knew it all," and she would feel she had not made progress.

I asked, "What comes to mind when you think of someone taking the credit for what belongs to you?"

She once more fell into a fighting mood. The calm of summer was gone. She screamed, "What comes to mind is my stupid, fucking father who made me a servant. He insisted I clean up all his messes. He would show me off to the world proudly and beam. Then when we were alone he displayed little care about what I truly felt."

She was silent a moment, but then raged on. "As I think about his narcissism and selfishness, I'd like to kick him in the balls."

For several sessions Nancy ranted and raved about her father's coldness. I just listened. Then one day, toward the end of September, she said thoughtfully, "And what's more, Strean, *you* never say anything nice to me. You *never* praise me. You sit in your chair and let me do all the work. I pay you money and I also do the work. It's damned unfair, don't you think?"

I still said nothing. She went on, "You've got it good. How come you don't let me decide when the vacation will be? You make the decision. You've got all the power. I have none."

Her conviction that I had "all the power" and she had none would consume many analytic hours during the months to come. It became a major issue in her life as she spoke constantly of feeling "powerless," while everyone around her possessed the "power."

I asked, "When you were in the mental hospitals, did you feel powerless in the presence of the psychiatrist who gave you injections?"

Her voice was low. "Oh, boy, did I. I used to beg each one, 'Please don't do this to me. It hurts too much. I will die. I have no way to fight back. You have all the power.' "

Power, for Nancy, meant many things. For one, power referred to the strength men had that she lacked. It also referred to the power anyone held over her when she could not get what she wanted. Her fantasy of power started early in childhood when she was informed of the "do's" and "don'ts" of existence by her mother. Nancy had to repress all resentments because her mother always felt ill, needed sympathy and caring.

Every patient in psychoanalysis (perhaps everyone alive) is involved in power struggles. Whenever we cannot have what we want, which is apt to occur almost every day, we resent those who frustrate us or the forces that impede and oppose us. All of us want health, wealth, love, fame, happiness, but the unalterable fact is that many of us do not achieve even a small fraction of what we desire.

The more we feel entitled to all kinds of gratifications, the more we feel disappointed and angry when we do not receive them, hence, the profound feeling of powerlessness. The emotionally disturbed patient, frustrated frequently in childhood and consistently over the years, feels naturally very "powerless."

His parents seem like harsh dictators, his siblings like demigods, and everyone and everything in the world seems bigger and better than he is. The murderous wishes the schizophrenic holds, which I saw clearly in Nancy, was a reaction to her feeling so deprived.

It does not take a very observant person to recognize how powerless the mental patient in a hospital ward feels when he blurts out, "I am Napoleon"—a defense against powerlessness by making himself a dictator who feels capable of conquering the world. The same defense is seen in the woman who proclaims, "I am Joan of Arc." This is a common delusion of women patients who wish to be as powerful as a man fighting for the freedom of his country.

Nancy was now slapping me, as she saw it, in the face in the way she dreamed she slapped the principal. She was retaliating for the power she felt I exerted, whereas she had none. It was helpful for her to feel the freedom to vent her rage, to feel safe in doing so. But I knew it was even more important to help her understand how and why she exaggerated my power and trivialized her own.

I was able to point out her distortions more clearly in

October when she had another dream. She pictured me holding a carrot. She then tried angrily to take it out of my hand and succeeded eventually in grabbing it for herself. As she ate the carrot, she grew larger and larger, like Alice in Wonderland.

"I became almost as tall as you," she said.

In reality I was five feet ten-and-a-half inches and she was five-feet-four but, in fantasy, what did this difference in size mean to Nancy? I asked, "What would it do for you to become as tall as I am?"

She replied swiftly, "I'd have your stature. I'd be a solid citizen, like you are."

With only mild hesitation she added, "And I'd also have balls. Then I could rule the world." Recalling words from childhood she quoted, " 'Balls,' said the queen. 'If I had two, I'd be king.' 'Balls,' said the king, because he had two."

I then asked Nancy, referring to her dream, "Why do you need a carrot to be like me? What don't you like about who you are?"

Nancy suddenly turned angry. She blasted me, "You can sit there with your smug, arrogant, shit-eater's grin and ask me what's tough about being a woman? You know goddam well you're better off than I am and always will be.

"Did you ever have to take shit from arrogant people? You were probably adored all your life. Did you ever have to be your father's slave? Your father and mother probably said, 'I love you, my son, the doctor.' Were you ever underpaid because you were a man? I overpay you and, if I were in your business, you know damn well I wouldn't get your fees. It's a man's world, an unfair world!"

A few times during her long tirade, she tried to provoke me to argue. I knew it was vital to keep out of verbal fights, for then we would be engaged in a power struggle. It is futile to try to help a patient through argument. He has to reach his own convictions via the analyst's interpretations and the empathy established between patient and analyst.

During a session in November, Nancy asked once again, "Don't you agree you're better off than any woman? Don't you feel women really are second-class citizens?"

More important than her words was the belligerent tone of her query. I responded, "You sound angry."

"I *am* angry," she said. "You sit back there gloating as I suffer and feel so inferior."

As is true with most patients who attack verbally, if the analyst does not join the argument but maintains a quiet interest, the patient begins to reveal the feelings, conflicts and despair that have stirred his rage.

It took me a long time to appreciate that when a patient, or nonpatient for that matter, becomes angry, he feels vulnerable and powerless. I went through many years of personal analysis to understand that beneath my angry thoughts and murderous fantasies lay feelings of weakness and vulnerability. I learned over the analytic years that my rage often hid fear and the wish to still be a little boy, taken care of by my mother and father.

Nancy described, in December 1982, a dream in which her right arm was severed and she became a bloody mess.

Her thoughts poured out with a richness of feeling. "As you've often pointed out, I must be feeling guilty for something when I arrange to have my arm cut off in a dream. It was my right arm, the one I use most. I must have felt *very* guilty."

She thought a moment, then went on, "I think I made my right arm 'wrong,' for wanting to do some 'wrong' things with it—like punching my father in the balls, and doing the same to my brother. I also wanted to hit my mother with my right arm as she lay dying, for being sick and deserting me when I needed her desperately.

"I know now she couldn't help falling sick, she wanted to live as much as I did. But as a child all I knew was that she wasn't there when I needed her. She just lay in bed day after day, moaning and groaning. And then suddenly she disappeared forever."

After another silence, she spoke in a reluctant tone. "I also remember as a girl masturbating with my right arm. I guess if you add the guilt about that to all the other reasons I mentioned, I feel my arm should be taken off so I can't do any more damage with it to my mind or body."

Nancy had alluded to masturbation a few times during her analysis but not in detail. It represented a conflict in her life that we needed to understand better. I asked, "When you masturbated, what were your fantasies?"

She thought for a moment, then said, "That I was growing a penis or had a penis."

As she described her wish to be a man sexually, it was still not clear why her arm (representing the penis) deserved to be amputated. The answer emerged the following month, in January, when after a few days' vacation, she told of another dream in which she and I were having sex on the couch. She pictured herself as possessing a penis while I had a vagina.

Following statements that showed her pleasure in being a man and possessing the coveted penis, I asked, "How do you suppose I felt without my penis, which you had?"

Without hesitation she replied, "I guess you'd be so angry at me that you would want to amputate my arm and get back your penis—turn me into a bloody mess."

This was her fantasy of how she obtained a penis, through warfare of the most savage kind. In some past battles, soldiers cut off an enemy's penis to show symbolically their power to destroy what they believed man's most precious possession.

Nancy was finally able to accept with conviction the main reason she demeaned herself and her vagina. She viewed it as a castrated penis and experienced her menstrual period as blood flowing from the wound following castration.

Her wish for a penis was not only the wish to be like her father but also her brother. Hence, her competition was twofold and her wish to castrate a strong one. In many ways she felt like a guilt-ridden criminal who needed to be punished for "evil" fantasies that had been deep-rooted for many years.

As Nancy talked about her envy of men and her wish to be a man, a number of problems she had never discussed now emerged. One afternoon in February 1983 she sounded euphoric as she said, "A problem I've had for years has disappeared."

Then she fell silent waiting for me to encourage her to

go on. I said not a word—by now she knew this meant, "Keep speaking."

She gave a nervous laugh, said, "The truth, my good doctor, is that I no longer suffer during my menstrual period. I'm sure it has a lot to do with the analysis, though I don't know why the pain has stopped so suddenly."

I was delighted to learn Nancy possessed one less problem. I believed the diminution of her menstrual pain had a great deal to do with what we were working on. Very often patients feel better in analysis but do not know why. Sometimes even the analyst does not know. Patients may also feel worse, which baffles both patient and analyst. As I have continually emphasized with students in analytic training, our job as analysts is to understand all psychic phenomena—for better or worse.

The mutual sharing with the patient of what happens within during analysis, what helps him feel better or worse, must take place. Otherwise the patient will continue to feel helpless when he leaves analysis. He will inevitably confront the same conflicts and confused thinking that has made him unhappy over the years.

I asked Nancy, after she told me of her pleasure in feeling free of menstrual pain, "What embarrassed you about telling me this?"

She paused, then said slowly, "Until you just asked me the question, I honestly didn't know. But now I think of my vagina. Something about your looking at my vagina bothers me."

There was a longer silence, then she went on, "You

probably want to know what bothers me when you're staring at my vagina. I am afraid you will see blood. And if you see blood, you'll know I'm a girl who had her penis yanked off."

She added ruefully, "When I was a little girl, my mother especially, but my father too, gave me the message I should never be elated for too long, no matter how much pleasure I felt in achievement."

It seemed characteristic of Nancy throughout the analysis and her life that, following every achievement or enjoyable experience, she thought of herself, as she put it, as "too cocky," or "having a cock that had to be amputated." Then she would feel deeply depressed, unworthy of any feeling of joy.

It did not surprise me, therefore, that in early March, following her jubilation at understanding why her menstrual cramps had vanished, she once again began to question herself and the analyst about her progress.

"I don't know what it is but again I feel we're not getting anywhere," she complained. "Sometimes I think this analysis works, only to plunge into disappointment, over and over again.

"I believe you know what you are doing most of the time, but often I don't really think you have much psychoanalytic understanding, Dr. Strean. Coming to see you these days is boring. I'd rather do something else—like write poetry, or go to the theater. Have some kind of fun."

At least she was considering "fun," I thought. This was a step forward, considering the depths of depression in which she had existed all her life.

"Last night I dreamed I walked into your office wearing a bright red dress," she said. "You made me change into a drab gray one. I stared at you in your handsome sports jacket, then told you that you should wear a torn sweater.

"You see what you do to me? I want to be happy and colorful and you try to make me morose and sad. And in the dream I feel angry at you for taking away my happiness. So I try to take away your attractive sports jacket."

I asked, "What are your associations to 'taking away' your happiness?"

After a moment of silence she laughed, said nothing.

I asked, "What's so humorous?"

With mild embarrassment she said, "When you talked about 'taking away' my happiness, I heard it as 'taking away my penis.' "

She equated "happiness" with "owning a penis," which then had to be "taken away." Nancy's envy of men was something she did not suffer alone—all women envy men and all men envy women—but the intensity of her envy and her power struggle was stronger than that of most of us.

Nancy's younger brother was favored from birth on—she received this message from both parents: "I wish you had been born a boy." This psychic wound was compounded by deep discomfort over her erotic feelings for her father and her mother's illness and eventual death. Nancy's oedipal conflict, a stage all girls pass through, was far too intense. As is true for any girl or boy who has strong incestuous fantasies and wishes to murder the parent of the same sex, attempts to move toward becoming a different gender seems a solution.

Such children have been overstimulated by circumstances that make them feel an oedipal winner, followed by deep guilt.

This was Nancy's plight, as it was Leonardo da Vinci's, who had no father and was left to the tender ministrations of a seductive mother. Leonardo believed he would be happier as a girl, just as Nancy felt she would be happier as a boy. When sexual wishes toward the parent of the opposite sex are very intense, as is the hostile competition with the parent of the same sex, children often renounce both sexual interest and hostile competition. Instead, they try the life of the opposite sex, believing they are safer.

Whenever a child cannot accept with pleasure his own sexual identity, he feels very angry, then very depressed, deprived of his real sense of self. Nancy felt angry much of the time and also depressed, not to mention devoid of a strong self. Thus it did not shock me in April 1983 to hear of another sexual symptom she found difficult to share with me until now. It, too, was related to her wish to be a man.

"It's more embarrassing than anything else to tell you what I've been doing since the age of ten or eleven," she confessed. "Even though I do it much less frequently these days."

I heard a deep sigh from the couch, then she said, "This analysis works, I now realize, because I have been able to give up not only my menstrual cramps but something else that has caused a lot of pain."

I did not dare guess what this was and her description startled me.

She said, gathering courage, "Ever since I've been a

little girl, I've shoplifted. Nothing really expensive—chocolate bars from the counter when I was in kindergarten, small
purses and perfume bottles recently. Then one day I asked
myself, 'Why do you still steal? It's against the law. If you
got caught you'd go to jail. Paul and Sheila would be horri-
fied.' "

She asked somewhat weakly, "Are you still going to love
me?"

I replied, "Once more you're all set for me to take
something away from you. You feel if you share with me
something like shoplifting I'll judge you negatively and take
away my love."

This was how she expected her parents to react—to
punish her for her transgressions. It was painful for Nancy,
as it would be for any patient, to accept that an analyst, rather
than punishing her for breaking the law, would try to help
her understand what unconscious fears and fantasies propelled her into such destructive behavior.

Feeling safer after several years of analysis, Nancy could
trust me enough to reveal acts she would never have dared
mention the first year of treatment. She was able to question
what lay behind her need to steal from stores.

What did shoplifting mean to her? The chocolate bars
to "small purses" and perfume bottles reflected her hungry
need for something "sweet" and "dark" as a child and the
equally hungry need for a vaginalike object and fragrant
scents as an adult. These combined fantasies that focused on
feces, hunger and feminine, alluring scents that would attract
men.

Nancy seemed ready to experience not only long-buried

memories but the feelings attached to them—an indispensable part of every analysis. Freud suggested early in his career that unless the hidden emotions were experienced, the analysis would not succeed. To this day, most analysts, if not all, agree the unconscious *must* be made conscious. Repressed feelings, hidden wishes and horrifying thoughts have to be consciously confronted.

Nancy said one afternoon, "I guess I've always felt deprived and when I felt gypped, I had to fill a big, empty vacuum."

In the earlier phases of analysis she lamented her "vacuum" without any insight. She now faced herself with more courage. She went on, "That vacuum is my vagina, isn't it? All the stuff I want to steal, that I 'yank out' or rip off from stores, are cocks I want for myself, that I feel driven to snatch from the owner.

"I guess it's similar to the dream where I took off that good-looking jacket you were wearing and replaced it with a ripped-up one. I did to you what I felt was done to me. I make you and the store owners ripped up and ripped off, so I can have something you don't have anymore."

As is true of every analysis, external events are always influencing the patient's state of mind. An analysis can never be just an examination of fantasies, memories, dreams and reactions to the analyst. Patients fall sick, their loved ones have difficulties, there may be a new baby in the house—everyone faces emotional ups and downs with family, friends and colleagues. These occurrences induce reactions in the patient that consume the analysis sometimes for weeks, even months.

In May 1983, an unexpected tragedy stirred Nancy deeply. Her father suffered a severe heart attack in his early seventies. She had drawn away from him after her marriage —he had not overtly disapproved but she knew he resented her living with another man.

She arrived at a session after a visit to her father as he lay dying. She looked gaunt, tired, as she slowly lay down on the couch. She said, her voice low, "I stared at my father stretched out on his bed, weak and old, his hair white. I thought, 'This time *he* is the patient and I am the helper, though there isn't much I can do.' The doctor told me he had only a few days to live."

She added, as she clutched a Kleenex, "Maybe because of the reversal of roles, I was able not to feel my usual resentment for being tormented and teased as a child. Instead I felt sympathy and understanding of his difficult life. He became a victim of sorts when my mother died so early and he was left to raise two children."

She was close to tears as she went on. "I never realized what a frightened man he was, I thought of him as God. But now I saw he probably was quite insecure and uncomfortable in whatever sexual life he had after my mother died. I felt very, very sorry for him as I could look back on his torment. Up to that moment, I had only thought of my own."

When a patient starts to feel empathy toward a parent who has been insensitive and inconsistent, the analyst knows the treatment is having a positive effect. As Nancy could accept herself more, psychic warts and all, she was far more understanding of the rest of the world. She moved from the stubborn position of a defiant child, furious because she was not understood, to that of a mature adult who felt less rage as she started to understand others suffered too.

She also told me, "I feel like taking care of my father and being his exclusive partner, kind of a substitute wife, like when I was a little girl. Yet I also feel angry because I have to take care of him as he lies helpless. I am supposed to mother him in a way I was never mothered. I feel sad, frustrated and depressed but not so overwhelmed as before I came here for help."

Like all patients, no matter how well analyzed, and like all of us, no matter our nature, when a crisis erupts we inevitably regress. How much effective analysis we had or how much maturity we enjoy will influence how we cope with the crisis.

Nancy became a little girl again, for the moment, as she reexperienced all kinds of sexual fantasies about her father when she saw him on his death bed. But these fantasies no longer overwhelmed her. She could accept them with equanimity and with far less guilt and anxiety. She could fantasy herself as a substitute wife without punishing herself too severely. She realized part of her would always remain her father's daughter. She could also now relive her mother's death with remorse and slight anger. As she put it, "What was, was. I can now mourn properly instead of blaming myself for her dying."

Nancy delivered the eulogy at her father's funeral. As she quoted from it in her analytic session, I found the words poignant and philosophical. She had memorized parts of it and her poetic imagery mesmerized me. I found myself in tears, which had only occurred three or four times in my long career as an analyst. As I analyzed my tearful response, I recalled a memory. When my sons were twelve and nine, I drove them to camp for the first time, their initial major separation from their mother and me. I walked down a hill with tears in my eyes, realized I was coping with deep feelings of loss. As I approached my car, the camp director saw me and called out, "Dr. Strean, could I have a moment with you?"

I dried my tears swiftly with a handkerchief, walked over to him. He said, "Doctor, some parents here are having trouble separating from their children. Do you have any advice?"

Frankly, I do not remember what I answered but I certainly did know I identified with the other parents, as I did now with Nancy's real loss.

Just as my two children were separating from me in memory, Nancy was separating from her father but also was showing me she could live more and more on her own. I sensed her growing away from me, much as my sons did in that camp scene.

This book, as I realized while writing it, is my way of holding on to the memory of Nancy. As I recall and review her sessions, I vicariously return to working with her. At the times I felt closest to Nancy, when progress was evident, the results rewarding, she seemed to some extent like a "benign mother" to me.

As I took notes on where Nancy stood psychologically (after she left her session), I saw her emerging into a far stronger woman, a person starting to show the capacity to feel a range of human emotions. She could now reflect on the past, not be overwhelmed and burdened by it. She was able to relinquish wishes that could never be gratified.

This is the true power—not the power she ascribed to a few inches of masculine flesh. The power she now experienced would give her far more pleasure than she thought only a penis could provide.

Nancy had wanted to control her father and brother, her husband and daughter, and then me. The person who needs to control is the frightened person. He has to control everything so he will not fall to pieces at life's small hazards and demands, which to him seem gargantuan.

Nancy had been in part controlled by cruel acts of fate, such as her mother dying and a dominating, seductive father. She fought to protect herself by controlling others, propelled by her fear of them. To her, power and control were one and the same. She had hoped they would lead to sanity but her need had become so excessive, instead they led to a sense of paranoia.

P   A   R

T IV

THE
FOURTH
YEAR

SPRING
1983

9

DREAMS THAT UNLOCK PSYCHIC TORTURE

Spring and Summer 1983

When Nancy freely described the thoughts that followed a dream, her secret wishes and her fantasies emerged as did her buried memories—memories she preferred to forget because she thought them shameful. As the unconscious meaning of the dream became conscious, she no longer had to expend precious energy repressing the supposed sins her dream concealed.

Dreams give a clue to the fears we hide. If a man who has sexual difficulties with women constantly dreams of his mother or a mother figure, we may infer he cannot enjoy himself with a woman because he still feels he is a small boy and suffers guilt over turning his partner into the sexually tabooed mother. Or if a patient suffers migraine headaches, insomnia and depression, his dreams may reveal angry power struggles with oppressive figures, which suggest that unconsciously he harbors deep sadistic wishes.

Since 1900, psychoanalysts and other therapists have used dreams to help patients understand what they have hidden from themselves over the years. Every dream, Freud pointed out in his classic *The Interpretation of Dreams*, conceals a secret wish and, as this wish is made conscious, the energy used to imprison it becomes freed for productive instead of destructive purposes.

Many a patient who suffers haunting inner obsessions no longer feels tormented when he understands the sadistic wishes of his dreams. The phobic patient, who must avoid what he believes "dangerous" situations, becomes less phobic when he discovers forbidden sexual fantasies that emerge from a dream. The patient who suffers psychosomatic illnesses, such as asthma, back pains and even the common cold, is able to give up the somatic symptoms as he discovers through his dreams that the symptom is his way of crying out for comforting love and maternal care.

Freud also pointed out that dreams preserve our sleep. When we lie down at night, whether aware of it or not, we place ourselves in the position of a regressed child as we assume a foetal position. The very inhibited cannot allow themselves to regress because they are unable to tolerate the passive wishes and childish fantasies that lying down induces. This is why the couch is used in psychoanalysis—to help the patient regress, get in touch emotionally with his long-buried childish wishes comprising the psychic engine that propels his unhappy, unknown inner life.

When we lie down at night and inevitably recall childish wishes of a sexual or aggressive nature, the dream also becomes a way of allowing us to sleep on. The dream often feels like a movie or television show we watch rather than a script we create. At first, most patients experience their dreams as imposed on them rather than arranged by them.

When forbidden wishes, such as incest or murder, become terrifying in a dream, we call this a "nightmare" and may wake in a panic or sweat. This is similar to going to a movie or watching a television show and finding that a scene of murder or sexual abuse is so upsetting we have to walk out of the theater or turn off the set.

When patients in analysis begin to accept they script their dreams—they alone arrange the action—they are on the road to accepting responsibility for their lives. As they acknowledge it is they who arrange the murder or the incestuous or sexually abusive scene, they take a further step along the "royal road" to a conscious awareness that will lessen the power of what they believe dangerous fantasies and fears.

As patients report their dreams in analysis, often the analyst becomes an important figure but usually in disguise. By helping the patient understand how he distorts the analyst in his dreams, the analyst helps the patient discover how he distorts his current relationships. He may turn a spouse into a punitive parent, a child into a competitive sibling, an employer into a tyrannical relative.

Early in analytic training I was told not to ask for dreams from a patient diagnosed as "schizophrenic." The rationale was that the very disturbed patient becomes terrified of the primitive dream feelings and feels even more emotionally disturbed if the dream is analyzed. This belief is still *au courant* in many psychiatric circles and even in some psychoanalytic ones.

Nancy, early in her analysis, told me that virtually all her therapeutic helpers had rejected the idea of looking at her dreams and thoughts as a way of relieving her misery. To the therapists this was like watching a frightening movie or terrifying TV drama they thought the patients would find confusing and overwhelming. To me, this was yet another indication of the profound fear many therapists show toward the schizophrenic patient.

I have reached the further conclusion that when one human being cannot bear something in another, he cannot tolerate what it stirs within himself. If a therapist cannot listen to a dream from a schizophrenic patient about incest, murder or sexual abuse, the therapist is frightened of his own incestuous, murderous or sexual thoughts and fantasies. This is, to some extent, true for patients less severely disturbed, if their dreams and free associations stir up such forbidden or frightening impulses in the therapist that he immediately shies away from the patients' dreams.

In supervising analysts-in-training for the past twenty

years, I have noted repeatedly that when they refuse to deal with material that is overtly or covertly expressed by patients, they are trying to escape their own anxieties and forbidden fantasies. They have not probed deeply enough in their personal analyses into buried fears and fantasies that still haunt them.

As I have suggested throughout this book, much of the treatment of the schizophrenic patient becomes a self-fulfilling prophecy. For instance, when a patient's dreams are rejected, he starts to feel rejected as a person. He wonders just how vulnerable or crazy he is. Then he starts to act in less rational ways. We see this constantly in areas outside psychotherapy. In educational circles, students are labeled incorrigible or uneducable and then slowly we watch them become antisocial delinquents.

I believe, by telling Nancy early in treatment I was interested in her dreams and wanted to work with her to understand their hidden meaning, this exerted a profound therapeutic effect. She began to feel I looked at her as one of my analytic patients, not as a "freak" schizophrenic. Slowly she became more similar to the fairly typical analytic patient, due to my belief she could be analyzed. Having had several experiences with schizophrenic patients prior to Nancy, from the moment I met her I treated her like a normal patient, not a "hopeless, crazy person."

When I say "treat her like a normal patient," not as a "hopeless, crazy person," I talk about a therapeutic attitude that, I believe, is helpful to all patients, regardless of diagnosis. While Nancy would have been diagnosed as an "ambulatory paranoid schizophrenic," the attitude to which I refer is based not on diagnosis but part of a philosophical stance toward all those in all therapies—outpatients and inpatients.

This attitude, perhaps more than many of my interpretations, proved of great therapeutic benefit. I believe that in all analytic work the analyst's positive attitude toward the patient is inevitably more crucial than the timing or content of any interpretation. If the patient feels the analyst has hope for him he starts to have respect for himself and hope for a happier future. In other words, the patient incorporates—psychically takes in—the analyst's attitudes, much as a child does his parents' feelings about him.

Just as most of us can spot a child who is loved and understood by his parents, those of us who are therapists can identify a patient who has been respected, loved and understood by his analyst. Just as all parents have their biases and feel more comfortable with certain behavior in their children, analysts have their biases and feel more at ease with certain patients.

By spring 1983 I felt quite relaxed as I worked with Nancy. I could identify with the intensity of her emotions because I could accept myself as an intense person. I believe the characteristics of Nancy that disturbed her previous therapists were her clinging manner, her constant demands and her belligerence—parts of myself I spent much time understanding and accepting in my analysis. Also, Nancy's dreams—filled with vivid colors and dramatic scenes—fascinated and stimulated me, for I dreamed in a similar way.

While Nancy had been able to carry on much of her own "dream analysis," she now described a series of dreams that, on careful scrutiny by both of us, had a deep impact on her thoughts and progress in analysis.

Just as Nancy could express herself poetically, her dreams frequently showed a poetic bent or a novel twist. In April 1983, she dreamed of a "monster" in a suitcase. She felt undecided whether to open the suitcase because, as she explained, "I was frightened what might come out."

Just as she had successfully revealed her thoughts about previous dreams, she told me (and her conscious self) what the monster represented: "He is part of me. He makes my demands as a child and shows the anger I felt when those demands were not fulfilled."

She went on, "You should know by now what a monster I can be. When I wanted to be your lover or your daughter or your baby, and you didn't take care of these needs, I felt like kicking you, beating you, clawing you. I always kept this rage silent because up to now no one would listen. I wanted to lash out and commit murder all my life and a buried part of me has known it."

She lapsed into silence a few seconds, then went on, "I could never reveal my rage to anyone. For many years I thought I killed my mother by showing her some of my resentment. I even thought my wanting to be mothered drove her crazy. I never felt my father was comfortable, either, in allowing me to express my feelings as a little girl. I've always hidden my wish to storm at him."

More silence. "I certainly could never scream at my brother or teachers or friends. All my angry feelings and wishes to be taken care of made me feel I was a monster.

And as I retreated more and more into myself and became depressed and agitated, those goddamn psychiatrists told me I should keep my yearnings buried, my anger subdued. Act like a normal person."

Through this dream, we see how and why someone can become a schizophrenic. When normal childhood wishes to be loved and understood are frustrated, as they were in Nancy's life, the child feels angry, then very guilty for being a child.

When parents are incapable of understanding a child's wishes to be held close, to be given to, to be understood, to be caressed, to be nurtured, the child believes his normal wishes are "evil," taboo, and must be repressed from consciousness and the world. He then becomes furious because he feels so frustrated and wants to lash out at everyone.

If the child cannot in some way discharge his hatred but must contain it, he becomes an emotional cripple, starved for love yet repudiating the wish for love. He is furious no love is available and also must hide his anger at this deprivation.

As Nancy was able to talk more about her hidden anger, she could see with far more clarity why she became so paranoid. One afternoon, stretched out now in comparative comfort on the couch, she said, "I understand why I have had so many fights all my life—at work, in my marriage and now with you. I have made the world my family and I want to fight it out all over the globe because I feel everyone is evil, wants to do me in."

When I asked Nancy her associations to the "suitcase" in her dream and why the monster appeared in it, she said, "A suitcase is for traveling." She thought for a moment, then explained, "Many times I wanted to pack a suitcase and run away from home. I would sit in my room, feel no one understood or supported me."

She added an important meaning to the "suitcase" as she remarked, "Psychoanalysis is also a journey. And I feel now I am ready to open up the suitcase of my mind and explore all the horror I have stored over the years that makes me feel I am a monster."

She spoke slowly, with deep conviction, "I still have some monstrous feelings toward you. You sometimes give me double messages that make me writhe in fury. You say, 'Tell me whatever is on your mind and I'll try to understand and help you.' This seems like a supreme act of love. But then you never do anything *except* listen and once in a while interpret. This makes me feel you really are a bastard."

Her voice rose in mild rage. "You have never once held my hand in sympathy. You never once have given me a warm hug of approval. You never once said you loved me. Sometimes I think you're a priest who just listens, maybe forgives but never shows any warmth physically."

I thought, This is the wrath of the little girl who was never given hugs of approval, never told she was loved, whose hand was never held in sympathy, who was never shown much, if any, warmth in a physical sense. She grew up facing a cold, distant, inhumane world.

As Nancy talked once again of her wishes to be my "little girl" and showed anger when I did not respond, I felt it was time to bring up one of the most difficult issues in her current life.

"What is so hard about being an adult woman with me

and in the rest of your life?" I asked. "So often you want to be my little girl or somebody else's little girl."

At first she was furious at this question. It frustrated her intense wish to be treated and loved like a child. She refused to answer directly but she did reveal the "monster" dream that in many ways responded to the question.

I recall one time in my own analysis when Reuben Fine asked, "Why do you keep such a distance from me? You seem afraid of intimacy." I had responded with a few thoughts, such as my wish to make my analyst my dominating father or my unempathic mother, but felt these were not the real reasons. The night after this session I dreamed I went to a movie by myself, saw my younger sister in the audience and avoided her.

Now I could answer my analyst's question at the next session. I had avoided acting like my sister with him. I was afraid of exposing the part of me that wanted to be a young girl, the daughter of my analyst. During childhood, I felt, like Nancy, that the grass was proverbially greener on the other side. Just as Nancy felt that her brother had it better, I believed that my sister was treated more favorably. A child also wants the complete love of his parents. Even the slightest show of affection toward a sibling will make the child feel he has lost his parents' love.

The dream revealed a secret I kept locked in my suitcase. The wish to be my analyst's daughter seemed a stimulating desire but also very taboo. When I could face the part of me that wanted to be my parents' daughter, I felt more liberated. I could understand why I did not want to accept the adult man in me, as Nancy was finding it difficult to accept the adult woman in her.

As I reflected on my dream, it helped me identify more with Nancy when she brought up another dream toward the end of May. She told me, "Last night I dreamed I looked at a figure of a Superman whose name was Norman." After her associations to this brief snatch of a dream, we better understood why she had kept herself a terrified little girl for so long.

She said, "I guess Superman is what I want to be. A super man. It's not enough for me to want to be a man. I have to be a *super* man. Since in my dream I name him 'Norman' and you've taught me initials are important, I guess I have to conclude that Norman is a male version of Nancy."

She paused, then went on, "I've always wanted to be the biggest and the best. I've always wanted to show up my brother and my father. In order to accept myself, I've felt I had to be perfect. Then maybe I could be a somebody, amount to something. Instead of always feeling like a frightened little girl."

I kept silent, waited for her to say more. She obliged. "I remember getting ninety-nine on a geometry exam but felt depressed for several weeks because one boy got a hundred. All my life I felt the pressure to be tall and strong and master everything. I have the wish to surpass my father, my brother, the damn principal of the school and you. I am driven to compete with all you big pricks."

Then, in a faint, childish voice, "Can't you see why being a little girl and staying a little girl is so much easier?"

Once again, Nancy, better than any textbook, explained

why people regress and emotionally become infants. She put into words the origin of many self-destructive behaviors such as addictions, the inability to work, perversions and attempted suicides.

All of us possess what analysts call "ego ideals," or as Dr. Karen Horney put it, "idealized self-images." We feel self love if we satisfy certain ideals we learned from parents, grandparents, teachers and friends. Some of us can like ourselves when we are altruistic, others when we earn a lot of money, still others when we are self-effacing, even masochistic. Many of us resemble Nancy, for we fantasy ourselves as omnipotent giants—supermen or wonder women.

Unfortunately, these ideals become projected onto others, including our marital partner, friends, children and colleagues. We believe we cannot be loved unless we live up to the "voices" of our idealized self, which we also demand in those to whom we are close. The more powerful we must be (as in Nancy's fantasy of becoming Superman), the more we wish to achieve, the more omnipotent we have to appear, the more perfect we believe we can be, then the more strain we will live under and the greater anger we will feel as we fail to live up to such unrealistic "ego ideals."

When Nancy wished to be Superman, she could not take the pressure and regressed to feeling like a little girl much of the time. If you examine the ideals of gamblers, alcoholics, suicidal persons, you discover they are trying futilely to live up to unrealistic ideals. They go through the same sequence of behavior noted in Nancy. They try madly to achieve their goal, are furious when they recognize their ideals cannot be attained, wish to kill and maim others in fantasy. They feel they live in an imperfect world, become guilty and depressed. They prefer to retreat to the mentality of a child or, more accurately, the world to which the schizophrenic retreats— the world of fantasy, dreams and nightmares.

The more painful reality seems, the deeper the wish to escape. When Nancy's reality appeared unbearable, she wanted to become Superman. But sustaining the role of Superman was far too difficult—actually impossible. Therefore she retreated to the world of a little girl though soon that became too humiliating and she returned once again to the Superman role. Her life swung back and forth in a vicious psychic cycle.

Many believe their dreams allow them to escape the harshness and cruelty of the real world but in this they are highly mistaken. The surface story of the dream may seem delightful, sometimes even joyous, but if we do our psychic homework we discover painful truths about the past. We become aware of our need to cling to what analysts call the "internal objects" (our childhood mother and father), whom we have internalized. They pull the strings of our thoughts and deeds as if we were puppets. Dr. Joseph Sandler of London, internationally known psychoanalyst, refers to "the dialogue with the ghost mother" that goes on in all of us.

Nancy in May brought a dream to analysis that was highly significant. She placed herself in Central Park, where she was staring at two figures on a seesaw. She said, "One was the monster I dreamed about a few weeks ago. Remember? He was in the suitcase. The other was Norman, the superman who appeared in a more recent dream."

She went on, "When the Norman person was 'up,' the monster was 'down.' And when the monster was 'up,' Norman was 'down.' They alternated as they swung back and forth."

After a short silence she said, with new confidence, "Those are the two sides of me. When one is up, the other is down, near the dirt. When one is more visible, the other is buried in my unconscious. Norman and the monster compete with each other, struggle against each other.

"Perhaps this represents the strong power struggles in me we have talked about. But what this dream also tells me is that I either have to be a superman or a little infant, a rather monstrous one. I see the world in black and white, though I know life really isn't like that. There are also shades of gray, as I am learning here."

Nancy would refer to this dream many times during the remaining course of her analysis. The dream mirrored her lifelong conflict of either needing to feel like an omnipotent giant superior to everyone else, or, if that did not work, the infant monster within, who sought a supermanlike parental figure who would take care of her, fulfill every demand, even ludicrous ones.

I believed that perhaps Nancy's most pressing and everpresent problem, one she found extremely difficult to understand and give up, was her wish to be a perfect superman or to find someone who would be Superman and take complete care of her. This is the wish we all possess, a wish that Freud said, in "Analysis, Terminable and Interminable," keeps all patients in treatment a long time.

Nancy's grandiose fantasies, her wishes to be omnipotent or to have an omnipotent god in her life, were especially intense. It took her a long time to diminish their intensity because she desperately hoped and, at times, believed they could be gratified. She clung to these fantasies to compensate for her equally strong feelings of weakness and vulnerability. She needed constant and consistent help in slowly accepting the fact she could not be a god, there were no human gods.

In contrast to psychoanalysis's Hollywood image, in which the patient has a sudden, dramatic insight and then his life drastically changes for the better, the analytic process is much like learning a new vocabulary, a foreign language or advanced mathematics. In order to master a new language or any other skill, even driving a car, the learner moves forward and backward as he makes mistakes. By definition, learning takes time. There are inevitably progressions and regressions, times of conviction and times of deep doubt.

Nancy was, fortunately, well motivated for psychoanalysis, enjoyed the learning process, basically wanted to change, feel happier. I believe analysts have not thought through carefully enough the exact reasons why an individual wants to learn the language of psychoanalysis and partake in its unique process.

Just as there are intelligent individuals who do not make good college students, there are brilliant persons who do not wish to experience psychoanalysis. One characteristic of Nancy, which I have seen in patients who used the analytic process well, was a strong curiosity, particularly about human relationships, and how past ones influence the present.

Why one person and not another is willing to face the long-buried fears, terrors and frightening wishes that analysis reveals is an interesting question. I believe people can absorb pain when they believe with some conviction that through the conscious awareness a painful revelation brings, they will feel a sense of relief. This does take a certain ego strength.

The man or woman who enters analysis usually has a greater quest for the truth than the one who rejects it. I have found that when someone believes ardently in religion or politics or is committed to some form of explanatory philosophy such as Existentialism, often psychoanalysis will not attract him.

I also believe those who seek therapists are more willing to trust in and learn from another person. If the idea of learning from someone else looms as frightening or the concept of trusting a stranger seems too difficult, psychotherapy will loom as frightening or impossible.

As Nancy herself said on several occasions about her analysis, "I look at this experience as a kind of surgery. At times it hurts. At times I feel overwhelmed. At times I feel very frightened. But somehow I keep hoping that it's all worthwhile."

In other words, Nancy had "hope." I believe that for a patient to stay in analysis and "work through" his buried conflicts he has to possess hope. Earlier, I discussed the need for the analyst to have "hope," which the patient then absorbs, but often a patient shows hope within himself—the reason he dares tackle temporary life on the couch.

Often, as Nancy worked through her problems, she not only compared analysis to surgery but to taking a course. She frequently referred to me as a teacher and at one point quoted Anna Freud, a teacher of children (like Nancy herself) before she became a therapist.

Anna Freud spoke of the "surroundings" of a child in the classroom (or the patient in therapy) provided by the

authority in charge, the teacher (or analyst) who offered hope
and empathy as the child (or patient) struggled with the difficult task of learning about the world (or his inner self).

During July as Nancy worked at trying to become less
of a superman and more of a mature adult, less of a little girl
and more of a woman, she suddenly became exasperated. I
realized her exasperation related to my impending summer
vacation shortly after her father's death the previous May—
now I, too, would be deserting her.

As August approached, her exasperation once again appeared close to, if not actually, psychotic. She told me she
could not sleep because of her fear of nightmares from which
she would awake screaming. She also felt apathetic toward
Paul and Sheila. She wondered if she really wanted to continue teaching children, thought of not returning to school in
September.

She even questioned whether analysis was worthwhile.
She said grimly, "Maybe I should try some other form of
therapy."

When a patient feels depressed and directly or indirectly
criticizes the analysis, we know the patient is experiencing
negative thoughts and feelings that stem from childhood,
though expressed toward the analyst.

I asked Nancy, "What bothers you these days about me?"

Without answering directly, she reported a dream in
which my office was splattered with shit. Then she fell silent,
as though she did not wish to speak on.

I said, "You're having a difficult time telling me what
is shitty about me and analysis."

She laughed lightly, then with slight embarrassment,

described a fantasy. She reported, "Right now I see myself as a young kid smearing the walls of this office with shit."

She fell into silence. I waited her out.

She went on, "I'd like to stick your head in a bucket of shit. To put it mildly, I hate your guts. All you do is analyze me. I want to become stronger than any woman in your life and then you'd love me, admire me. But you never let me *be* the most important woman in your life. And you imply that being powerful is to be crazy. I hate you for that. When my hatred doesn't impress you, I try to make you into the father I never had but you don't let me do that either. I just hate your guts."

My hypothesis that her hatred would always explode in July was to some extent validated when she said indignantly, "It's always at this time of year, when you go away on vacation, that I realize how much I hate you. You never take me with you. I feel that if you loved me, you wouldn't leave me."

Silence, then: "You remind me of my parents, who abandoned me and enjoyed their own good times in Europe."

She asked, in more adult tone, "Are you going to Europe this summer? I wouldn't be surprised if you were. You're selfish and narcissistic like my mother and father. You give me next to nothing."

I thought, after one similar session in late July 1983, I give this woman much of my time and energy—when the hell is she going to start to mature, become more self-sufficient?

I thought of the mother of my childhood who never seemed fully satisfied no matter how hard I tried to please her. I felt as a child there was something wrong with me, if only I could be a better boy, a better son, my mother would smile more, be more satisfied, more loving.

As I reflected on these thoughts, which came to mind often while working with Nancy, I realized that just as Nancy wanted to be Norman, the superman, so had I. I referred to these thoughts as my "Herbert Sigmund Freud fantasies," believing I could cure schizophrenia quickly and easily—as unrealistic a fantasy as some of Nancy's.

I further recognized some of the irritation and impatience I felt that July made me more empathic toward the many colleagues who gave up on patients like Nancy. You are placed in a difficult situation with such a patient. No matter how hard you work and how disciplined you are, the patient, even after several hundred hours of therapy, looks upon you as a narcissistic, selfish son-of-a-bitch (as he did his mother and father). While I could tell myself Nancy's father had emerged as quite a selfish man, this knowledge did not fully compensate for the lack of what I wanted from Nancy—a slight degree of appreciation, of recognition, perhaps even admiration for my hard work.

Every analyst must be extremely vigilant in handling the child within himself, not let that child interfere with the patient's progress, as I have pointed out. Any time I feel angry at a patient, as I occasionally did with Nancy, I first had to accept my anger, then discover what the child in me was angry about. The more I could accept that child (one that never disappears but can be understood and controlled), the better analyst I would be. I have often recommended this to friends and family members. I urge, "Talk to the child in yourself—you'll be a happier adult."

During this July I realized again how similar Nancy and I were. Though her background was far more traumatic, she and I both had strong omnipotent fantasies to monitor in order to live more comfortably in the world of reality. Nancy and I were much alike. We both had to learn that though we felt misunderstood by our parents and others, we could never change the past but had to accept it as part of our lives. We had to diminish the power of our revengeful thoughts, accept ourselves more as adults rather than angry, hurt, mistreated children.

I recalled the many times students and supervisees who worked with patients who were schizophrenic, would tell me, "It's hard to understand this patient because I have nothing in common with him." In effect, they were denying their similarities.

When I was a graduate student and lived in a mental hospital, I had a maintenance scholarship and received room and board. I felt embarrassed one day when one of the inmates, the woman who cleaned my room, told me, "You and I have a lot in common. We're both reading the same book. I saw on your desk a copy of Lucy Freeman's *Fight Against Fears*, the story of her psychoanalysis."

I was embarrassed because this patient and I were obviously both interested in fighting our own fears. She also told me, "I often dream some of the same dreams Miss Freeman had."

I trusted Nancy would enjoy the vacation offered her in the coming month of August. She had made enough progress to feel more at ease during the few weeks lacking an analytic session.

Thus I left for the Adirondacks with far less trepidation than on our previous separations. This time I felt it was no longer a question but a certainty that I could count on her vast improvement in the past three and one-half years to carry her through the month without me.

10
THE
MURDER
WITHIN

**Fall
1983**

I was surprised to learn that the summer separation proved far more difficult for Nancy than I anticipated. In contrast to the summers of 1981 and 1982, in which she functioned reasonably well, this summer seemed traumatic. Nancy walked into the office in the fall feeling deep rage at me and analysis.

She told friends, relatives and colleagues during the vacation that psychoanalysis did not work. She left messages on my phone announcing she intended to quit treatment. Many of these messages sounded like infantile temper tantrums— protests at my not caring about her and at treatment as a whole. There was also disjointed thinking that included swearing, with many expletives in one sentence. Nancy appeared natural but the symptoms of illness had returned to some degree.

Even though I was aware of Nancy's "transference" love, my heart beat faster as her threats mounted. I felt a combination of feelings—stimulated because this attractive woman desired me so deeply, frustrated because I knew I could never get involved sexually with her and angry, because she was trying to manipulate me.

Her heated tone and intense demanding attitude also brought to the surface a feeling I had as a boy with my own, at times, hysterical mother. I felt as if my mother had threatened, "Herby, do what I say or you'll be in deep trouble!"

Nancy's threats reminded me particularly of a stage in my preadolescence when my mother threatened to send me to an institution for delinquent boys if I did not heed her admonitions. Nancy was threatening to send me to an "institution" for incompetent psychoanalysts.

As I reviewed what I felt, which always dissipates tension in me, I started to think about where Nancy now stood psychologically and why her demands seemed more intense than those of any other patient with whom I had worked over the previous three and a half decades.

I knew that schizophrenia takes many shapes and forms.

There is the extremely regressed schizophrenic patient we see in a mental hospital whose speech makes no sense. I recall a patient who uttered sentences such as, "My boat is flying high. The sound and the war are stupid. God bless Timbuctoo." Some patients do not even connect one word to the next and make no sense at all. This is known as "word salad," implying that thoughts and feelings are confusing to the speaker. Life, sentences, thoughts, words, become a maze in his mind.

While this deep regression in communication is extremely difficult to work with, there exists the even deeper form that appears in catatonic schizophrenia. The patient may roll up into a ball like a foetus in the womb. He refuses to eat or talk, sits mute like a dead body. He appears to have given up on life completely. The catatonic schizophrenic sees the world as a horrifying war in which he has no chance to escape alive, in which there is no one to protect him.

The less regressed patient, the one who speaks in the "word salad," is saying, "It is terrifying and dangerous to become an adult. I'll feel a lot safer if I speak like a one-and-a-half-year-old infant who doesn't know subjects from predicates." Such a patient does not feel as forlorn as the catatonic, who has given up, but his fear of danger is pronounced.

The patient who speaks in a "word salad" is terrified to use adult speech. He believes his aggressive and sexual thoughts will cause deep trouble if expressed. Thus he regresses to the speech of an infant who can cause no trouble since he cannot be understood. When someone is this terrified of his violent and/or sexual wishes, and what may happen if such thoughts are expressed, an incomprehensible "word salad" is his best defense—a magical compromise.

An important step in understanding the form and shape schizophrenia takes is to get in touch with the degree of terror and sense of danger in the person's life. The greater the terror and fear of danger, the more he is apt to regress. Such dangers usually stem from experiences at an early age with the parents, colored by the person's fantasies and distortions.

A child may be threatened from time to time by a raging mother or father, "I'll kill you for that!" and the child will take this literally, believe he will soon die. He may retreat from life, become psychically "dead" to avoid further threats and battle. This occurs in the autistic child.

As I have said, with Nancy's analysis she appeared as an average neurotic about eighty percent of the time. She came to four sessions a week, seemed to show growing inner security. She used regressive speech sparingly, such as the few times she called me "Mommy Herby" or when she "gooed" and "gaaed" gutterally like an infant at the breast.

But for most of the analysis she spoke quite intelligently, as I have reported. Nevertheless I would have to refer to her, in technical terms, as an "ambulatory schizophrenic" because at times her testing of reality was poor, her judgment shaky and her demands on others very unrealistic. Her paranoia, such as her occasional conviction that people, including me, were out to persecute, punish, hate her, could be quite intense.

From time to time I asked myself, "How can a woman like Nancy, who has been in mental hospitals, who was severely paranoid, who suffered hallucinations and deliriums, teach school?" Many wonder how a schizophrenic patient could possibly be a teacher, believing erroneously that schizophrenia is a disease that affects the person's ability to function and exists at all times.

This is misunderstanding the nature of schizophrenia. The schizophrenic person, I reiterate, is more similar to the average person than we realize. Just as the "normal" person has strengths and limitations, so does the man or woman we label "schizophrenic"—unless, of course, he suffers actual brain damage, which is physical not psychological.

I believe that both the mental health profession and the general public stereotype the schizophrenic when they believe he is completely crazy every moment of the day and night. If we view someone in this way we do not permit his sanity and strengths to emerge—which, unfortunately, occurs daily in mental hospitals. We hear repeatedly that certain schizophrenics are always irrational, never show signs of being sane. I am convinced most of those who work with and observe schizophrenics believe they are incapable of showing talents and skills and thus relate to them in a way that never permits these strengths to emerge.

There are certain cases where emotional damage in childhood at the hands of vicious, terrorizing, punitive parents has been so overwhelming that a schizophrenic becomes dangerous, cannot control his behavior and must be kept apart. This was the case of Joseph Kallinger, graphically described in *The Shoemaker* by Flora Rheta Schreiber. They became friends as she interviewed him, he told her he loved her as if she were his "good" mother, but warned her never to be alone in a room with him for he might kill her. He had committed three murders after hearing "voices" commanding him to kill, usually the voice of "God" or an inner voice called "Charlie."

Most schizophrenics do not have parents as brutal as Kallinger's, they received at least some degree of love and care. They do not commit murder except perhaps psychological murder of the self.

Despite the chaos in Nancy's childhood and adolescence, she was frequently rewarded for her outstanding academic work (one reason she could so easily accept the role of schoolteacher). Her teachers, as well as her father, thought her a very bright young girl. This part of her life was far less conflicted than, for instance, her relationships with men and women. Just as she had received positive responses in this educational area, she could give children positive responses in the classroom.

When Nancy was involved, however, in a close one-to-one relationship with a child, such as her daughter, her resentments toward her own mother might emerge. She sometimes found herself feeling helpless and hopeless in the presence of Sheila. But as Nancy could face more of the child in herself—the angry, demanding child—she found it easier to be with Sheila, talk to her, hug her, say she loved her.

There was a great contrast in behavior and attitude between Nancy as a teacher and Nancy as a wife. Because of her strong competition with her brother and her feeling of being teased and tormented by her father, she sometimes lived as if her husband did not exist. In much the same way, she felt she did not exist in the minds of the important people in her early life.

Many times in the course of analysis I asked Nancy, "How can you go for weeks without any mention of Paul?"

"I don't know," she said. "His name just doesn't occur to me when I am with you."

Eventually she realized she wanted me to be the only man in her life because she wanted to be the only woman in mine. The more she could accept the fact that a symbiotic relationship between her and her analyst was impossible, the more she could allow herself to see Paul as he was—a bright, caring, intelligent, though occasionally anxious man who appeared to love her in spite of her difficulty in accepting past hurts.

I knew Nancy's relationship with Paul had improved when she told me he stopped using the word "crazy" about her. At times he had told her he loved her even though he thought some of her behavior was "crazy." He said, "You remind me of my mother when you act that way." It was no accident he had selected as wife a woman much like his mother—as Nancy had selected a man somewhat like her father, successful in his chosen profession but having difficulty understanding her.

One of the issues every analyst faces, particularly when the patient is of the opposite sex, is that his being idealized and exalted does not necessarily forward analysis. To the contrary, if an analyst does not help a patient see him as he is—mortal, like everyone else, making mistakes at times and hating as well as loving—the patient will never understand reality, accept his own strengths and limitations.

I was fortunate in my own personal analysis in being helped to give up the idealization of my analyst. He encouraged me to face his limitations as a human being, thus I learned early in my career to help patients see me as I am. A few times with Nancy I enjoyed believing I was the man in her life but, just like the times I felt angry with her, I examined my feelings, did not let them interfere with the treatment.

I cannot stress enough the need for the analyst to be aware of his emotions, whatever they are. This awareness allows him to cope with his feelings so he does not dilute or destroy the therapeutic process.

I believed that giving Nancy the opportunity of four sessions a week, in which she could talk about anything she chose and attack me verbally in any way she wished, would help prevent her from regressing as much as in the past. I appeared less dangerous than the psychiatrists and other personnel in mental hospitals and elsewhere she had seen.

Her major way of dealing with danger was to attack. The more helpless she perceived herself, the more unloved and abandoned she felt, the more ungratified she remained, the more she wished to hurt others. I believe an infantile fear of horrifying danger leads men and women to commit murder. They cannot control the violent and sexual feelings that, as children, were stirred to a dangerous degree.

I think Nancy's choice of attack as a way of survival originated in many sources. First, she was a very sensitive child, alert to the feelings of her very sick mother and dominating father. Second, she was born with much energy, which she displayed in her current life—what child psychologists call "high-drive endowment." Third, she experienced her childhood, and life thereafter, as one big battle, remaining furious at her ungiving, dying mother and hostile father.

In my work with Nancy I learned that when she was most furious she felt most terrified, most endangered. Consequently, even before we resumed our work in fall 1983, I asked myself, What terror now provokes Nancy's extreme rage?

She had spent the summer carrying on a vendetta against analysis and me. She appeared like the classical paranoid schizophrenic who collects injustices and tries to muster an army of people to combat the enemy. I wondered why Nancy was experiencing me all of a sudden as the enemy.

I always feel a tinge of disappointment when a patient backslides, despite the fact I know this is par for the course of therapy. Even when my own personal analysis was well advanced, it was never easy for me to tolerate signs that indicated little or no progress. One of the most difficult lessons I had to learn as both analyst and human being was that lack of forward movement at times is part of every human experience. No interpersonal relationship—whether it be marriage, parent-child, friendship or work—only moves forward.

But having seen Nancy for over three years, it was, in spite of all my self-understanding and professional knowledge, difficult for me to be greeted by her in September 1983, with an extremely hostile frown and contemptuous sneer.

She had called me in advance to say she wanted to quit

analysis, did not intend to show up for her first appointment. I replied, "Before you make a final decision, it might be helpful to spend a few sessions talking it over."

She agreed to show up but before ending the conversation she warned, "You'll never convince me to stay."

Now, lying on the couch, Nancy held back her rage. She sounded more like an attorney dispassionately arguing a case or a philosopher disputing a theory, as she announced, "I have been doing a lot of thinking about this business of psychoanalysis and I have come to the conclusion it has no validity."

She went on in the same even tone, "Freud was a bright man but obsessed with sex. I am further convinced he was afraid of people and spent more time writing and reading than helping patients. He was not a humanitarian but a sexual pervert. And he encouraged egocentric, sexually perverse people like yourself to enter this inhumane profession."

The words were in contrast to an earlier phase in her analysis when she read Freud passionately and praised him. Now she studied him to crucify him. This mirrored her transference to me. She loved me in the past but now hated me, wanted to get rid of me.

It was clear Nancy harbored a deep murderous rage toward me. It emerged in such an intellectual way I was convinced that to respond would only lead to an argument rather than uncovering the feelings that were making Nancy seem paranoid and murderous.

I chose to keep quiet. The more silent I was, the more Nancy would have an opportunity to reveal to me and herself what upset her so deeply.

Often people imagine the analyst as someone who sits behind the couch and says little or nothing—a stereotype that has a great deal of truth. Analysts and other therapists who volunteer to help troubled souls know that the more they listen, the quieter they are, the easier it is for the patient to reveal his long-repressed feelings and thoughts.

While patients sometimes get angry at the analyst's silence, most eventually realize they say more and discover more about themselves when they freely associate to an attentive but quiet listener. As the patient progresses in analysis, he learns that the analyst will speak at the appropriate time—he has not disappeared or died.

So Nancy went on berating me in eloquent terms. However, I noticed she cursed less than before, appeared more as if she was my teacher and I, her incompetent student. She said, "You seem to have chosen a profession that gives you a lot of neurotic gratification. You confirm your theories but don't give a damn about your patient. You select your vacations without giving credence to your patient's needs. You impose all your ideas without listening to what your patients say."

As she continued to derogate and demean me, I had several thoughts. First, except for late August when she left phone messages in which she threatened to leave analysis, she still arrived for her sessions. Thus I inferred she gained some gratification and/or protection from being in my presence and tearing me down.

Furthermore, as I listened carefully to her accusations, one central theme emerged. Repeatedly she told me I was a selfish, inconsiderate, narcissistic, inhumane human being —personally and professionally.

My task at this time was to try to determine what motivated her, at this moment in treatment, to eloquently complain that I, like the important people in her life—mother, father, brother, husband—was a selfish egotist.

My quiet listening yielded a consistent theme, I could now intervene. After three weeks of almost complete silence on my part, I said to Nancy, "Throughout my vacation and since I have returned, you have experienced me as a very selfish, uncaring person."

Without directly responding to my words, Nancy described a dream the previous night: "I don't know if this dream has anything to do with what you just said. But here goes. I was teaching school, watching a little girl in kindergarten. She wanted to play with crayons and also wanted the teacher to watch her. The teacher got angry and made the girl throw away the crayons. At this, I woke up in a rage."

After a moment of silence she went on, "That teacher was selfish and egotistical. She wouldn't let the child do what was age-appropriate—to play freely. Instead she squelched the child's spontaneity and pushed her to conform to the teacher's excessively harsh standards."

I said, "What comes to your mind when you think of a little girl wanting the full attention of a teacher and not getting it?"

She responded at once, "You're the goddamn teacher who's a selfish bastard and I guess I'm the child who's being stopped from doing what comes naturally. I want to play and you won't let me. I want to be myself but you force me to do

otherwise. I know, you bastard, you'll say this is all transference. You're just like my mother whose needs I had to
take care of. And just like my father who gave me the same
kind of bullshit.

"Over the summer I couldn't enjoy my vacation because
I kept thinking of you, the harsh taskmaster who keeps saying,
'Work, work, work.' I want to play. I wanted to play on my
vacation but the image of you stopped me."

Here I could identify with Nancy, for one of my neuroses,
as both child and adult, was the conviction I had to work all
the time. Play was prohibited. It took many years of personal
analysis before I could enjoy a vacation—and even more time
until I could relax without writing articles or books.

Like Nancy, I felt that to esteem myself I had to placate
the voices of parents that ordered, Work, work, work. My
mother often said to me, "All play and no work makes Herby
a dumb boy"—a revision of "All work and no play makes
Johnny a dull boy."

I was tempted at this point in Nancy's therapy to say,
"All work and no play makes Nancy a dull girl" but this
cliché would not resolve her conflicts. Rather, Nancy needed
to learn that every time she wanted to play and did not, she
was maintaining a battle with her parents. She still was very
frightened of her normal wishes to "play." She needed to
learn that fantasies and wishes involving "play" had been
unduly terrorizing. She had arranged for me, like the internalized voices of her parents, to stop her from desiring forbidden moments of "play," which come naturally to a child.

It is extremely important to remember that in Nancy's
case, for her to "play" while her mother was dying represented

a sacrilege. She was forced to act grown up far too early in her life. She had to suppress her wishes to be like other children and suffer the toll of schizophrenia in later life because of her consummate emotional deprivation and subsequent rage.

When I asked Nancy what thoughts she had about my insisting that she "work, work, work" all the time, particularly during the summer months when I was ostensibly having "fun," she said, "Like my parents, you, Strean, are afraid to watch a child play. Maybe you, like my parents, and their parents, and their parents' parents, were told that play is something frivolous and should be denied a child.

"Maybe you, as a child, were inhibited from playing. Maybe you're against it because you can't tolerate it in yourself."

While her accusation could be labeled as "transference"—making me the parents who prohibited her from playing as a child—there was a certain truth to her paranoid accusations, as there often is to even the most disturbed patient's "injustice-collecting," as analysts call it.

I believe that on some level Nancy recognized I was at times a compulsive workhorse. While she was berating me for my resistance to play, I recalled a scene from "play therapy" with a four-year-old boy about twenty-five years before. He suddenly turned to me and said, "Dr. Strean, you work too hard. Let's just play." A brilliant prescription, I thought, then and now.

My association to this child patient helped me recognize what Nancy was trying to tell me during the past month. She wanted to play with me on vacation, but was too frightened to admit this to herself or tell me. Perhaps my championing of the work ethic exacerbated her resistance. But it was quite clear from her associations and from my own private ones that she really wanted to be with me, and me alone, vacationing in some quiet spot.

I said, "I think you're very angry at me because you would have liked to have been on vacation with me—and play with me like the little girl in your dream wanted to play with the crayons. But you feel I'm against play so you hate me for it."

She quickly replied, "You know what I want but you never give it to me. I'd like to take some crayons and smear you with them. What a cruel bastard you are—knowing what I want—to relax and play with you. Instead, you give me nothing."

Nancy was now in touch with her basic rage. She wanted me to be the mother, father and lover she never had, to play with her in a relaxed way. Instead, all I gave her were analytic interpretations.

"Play" also connoted sexual play and Nancy soon was able to tell me, "A few times during the summer I had the fantasy of lying on the beach with you and at least enjoying foreplay. But you're such an uptight creep I couldn't let the fantasy go on. You're always stopping me and saying, 'Work, work, work!' "

I began to realize that whatever my limitations, when it came to relaxing, Nancy had difficulty even imagining herself in a playful position with me. I felt it important to help her resolve her inhibitions and understand what really scared her about playing.

Thus, in late October I asked, "What do you think is so frightening about the fantasy of playing with me?"

She responded, in almost a joyous voice, "I didn't think you had it in you to fantasy playing with me."

But her initial enthusiasm was soon squelched as she then retreated into a long silence. Now I could say, "Just as it is dangerous to consider playing with me, you have to stop yourself from revealing your thoughts about what 'play' means to you."

This seemed to give Nancy the permission she needed. She started to verbalize her fears about the dangers of "play." She began to reach some of the fantasies inherent in the word "play."

She said ruefully, "Sometimes I felt I was forty years old when I was four. The only way I could be accepted was if I produced. I went on to become a good student, brought home high marks. All the teachers complimented me. I felt that unless I gave up my wish to play, I would be completely rejected."

Nancy then spent many sessions talking of her deep rage at not being able to enjoy a child's spontaneous play. She said angrily, "I feel like murdering everyone who stopped me from being a little girl." She described fantasies of destroying her father, others involving her mother, whose illness meant Nancy could never enjoy fun and frolic.

Then, as usually happens in most analyses, she again turned her analyst into the enemy-parent. She accused, "You never let me be a little girl. I always have to put out for you.

If I didn't give you lots of dreams, lots of fantasies, lots of history about my personal life and my interpretations, you'd hate my guts."

She then asked, "What would happen if I came here and gave you nothing? Wouldn't you throw me out after a while?"

Before I could answer, she told me of a fantasy she had as she taxied to the session. She said, "I saw myself as a little girl, about three or four, in your office doing 'play therapy.' I was finger-painting and enjoying it, but suddenly, in the middle of the fun, you stopped me."

She proceeded to demean and debase me for being a punitive play therapist. I felt she was now sufficiently secure in her analysis for me to ask, "Since this was your fantasy, why do you suppose you arranged for me to stop your play?"

After a few words of mild criticism, she explained, "If I really let myself go with the finger paints, I would act out here in the office what I did in one of my dreams. I'd dump the paints all over the place and shit all over you. I don't know what the exact truth is, but I think I was toilet-trained before I was less than a year old. I didn't even get a chance to shit and piss like a normal child. I remember my father telling me proudly what a wonderful little person I was for learning to control my bodily functions with such dexterity." There was sarcasm in her voice.

"I think the bastard took comfort in seeing me control myself in bathroom functions," she continued vehemently. "He thought he wouldn't have been a proper father if he'd let me do what comes naturally in the first two years of life."

In a sadder tone she added, "I know now why I loved

the song 'Doing What Comes Naturally.' If someone could have sung it to me and meant it, what a difference that would have made."

She was implying that she wished there had been fewer restraints on her natural impulses, that it was cruel to toilet-train her at least a year and a half earlier than the average child. Too-early toilet training invariably inhibits a child at a time his body is not ready to control elimination functions, but he feels compelled to do so in order to win a parent's love. When a child is stopped from "doing what comes naturally" too early, he will develop a very punitive conscience, restrict himself from many pleasures and always be on the lookout for attack. The paranoid person always expects a dangerous attack *from behind* (the anticipated spanking from childhood).

As she began to understand why she inhibited and re-strained herself, Nancy tried out new possibilities in her dreams and fantasies. Though she had made some attempts earlier in analysis to be a playful child, she now felt safe to experiment further.

She brought in dreams and fantasies in which she was the little girl and I was "Big Daddy," encouraging her to enjoy the sand, use finger paints and even, once or twice, dare to play with feces. She was trying, on the one hand, to give herself more pleasure, to be an unfettered infant again, but on the other was always on the lookout for my punishment.

This became even clearer one session during November when she dropped her purse and lipstick, rouge, wallet, Klee-nex and pen spilled all over the floor as she started to lie down on the couch. She looked at me with embarrassment and shame.

I said nothing, wanting her reactions. She seemed astonished and exclaimed, "Aren't you going to yell at me for being such a slob? Aren't you at least thinking what a messy girl I am?"

As she picked up the contents of her purse she kept taunting, "Don't you want to punish me for being so careless?"

I said, "You persist in wanting to be punished when you don't exert perfect control over yourself."

She responded, now lying on the couch and feeling more at ease, "I guess I keep being astonished by your message that I don't have to be a very controlled, obedient girl to get your love."

Nancy had been extremely revealing in telling me she did not have to be "a very controlled, obedient girl" to get my love. I thought, Her punitive conscience is loosening, her self-esteem increasing.

I recalled a time in my personal analysis when I could say something quite similar to my analyst. Like all patients, I made Reuben Fine into my parents in many ways, frequently viewed him as taskmaster. In one session I said something similar to what Nancy had just said to me, when I remarked, "You mean if I don't write a book a year, you'll still respect me?" This accomplishment seemed equal to getting hundreds and A-pluses and hitting home runs, which my father demanded, while also conforming to my mother's adage, "All play and no work makes Herby a dumb boy."

Had I not come to grips with this issue in my life, I

would not have been able to help Nancy play more freely. I thought at this time of Freud's well-known admonition to psychoanalysts: "You can only help a patient resolve the problems that *you* have resolved."

As much as Nancy was making progress in approving of herself, as Christmas festivities ended and we entered 1984, there was far more to be analyzed in the area of "forbidden play." In one dream I heard further of her inhibitions revealed.

"I was in a doctor's office and the doctor looked a lot like you," she said. "His name was Dr. Finger. He asked about the pleasure I got from sex."

This dream stimulated Nancy to share a secret difficult for her to expose, even though the analysis was now nearly four years old. She spoke of an almost lifelong "problem" with chronic masturbation.

She admitted, in apologetic tone, "Ever since I've been a little girl I have masturbated at least once a day, sometimes two or three times. Even when Paul and I have sex at night, I can't seem to stop. It's a deep need. He doesn't stay in me long and maybe this causes my hunger."

Nancy frequently referred to masturbation as a "problem" because she was so conflicted about it. On the one hand, she enjoyed the sexual stimulation and the fantasies as well as the orgasm. But she felt, as many men, women, children and adolescents do, that giving herself sexual pleasure was perverse and thus deserved punishment.

I encouraged Nancy to talk of her feelings and fantasies, to free-associate to her thoughts during masturbation. The analyst is never judge, he will not tell a patient whether an act or thought is "good" or "bad." Like most patients, Nancy eventually identified with my nonjudgmental attitude, made it part of her thinking and became more accepting of normal sexual wishes.

She seemed relieved to finally confess this dark secret. Embarrassed about a compulsion of which she felt ashamed, she had never told anyone, feeling it forbidden. She showed guilt about her confession as she described the repetitive fantasy she dreamed up while she masturbated.

"I imagine I am having sex with a belligerent man who beats me. I scream and try to kick him in the testicles."

Nancy's fantasy of being beaten by a man while masturbating is a common one for women. Freud studied what he called "erotized aggression" and the role of beating fantasies in perversion, character and the forming of symptoms in his classic paper "A Child Is Being Beaten: A Contribution to the Study of the Origin of Sexual Perversions."

He noted beating fantasies began early in life, were accompanied by feelings of pleasure and the climax of the imaginary beating situation was associated with masturbatory satisfaction. He said there were many causes for the beating fantasy, from oedipal love, guilt and masochistic excitement to a painful kind of mourning the lack of a sexual partner.

Freud just started to recognize the importance of aggression as a factor in its own right, as Dr. Harold P. Blum points out in his article "Paranoia and Beating Fantasy: An Inquiry into the Psychoanalytic Theory of Paranoia," published in the *Journal of the American Psychoanalytic Association* (Vol. 28, 1980, No. 2).

Freud recognized the paranoid person "as violently angry, afraid of his own aggression, and unconsciously wishing and anticipating attack. Hostility was reinforced and rationalized by the patient's exquisite sensitivity to the other person's hostile impulses and by the paranoid's actual provocation of hostile and punitive reactions in others."

Nancy as she masturbated, in fantasy, was engaging in a sadomasochistic orgy. I helped her understand why she held back this important information so long. Often patient and analyst learn more about the patient's inner life when the reasons for maintaining secrets come to conscious awareness and are analyzed.

All those in analysis possess secrets. Not a patient in the world is free from several or more secrets he fears to reveal to anyone. It is the secrets we try to hide from everyone that make us feel guilty and unacceptable, cause inner distress.

Actually, four years is not a long time to withhold a secret from an analyst. I have worked with patients who have kept secrets from me much longer. Their guilt ran too deep, their embarrassment was too severe. When you tell a secret, you also feel you have to give up the "forbidden" and part of you does not want to do this.

Nancy's reasons for keeping her secret were very revealing. "I told you how much 'play' has been forbidden in my life. I'm positive you've been against play. Surely you would be against the idea of my playing sexually with myself," she explained.

I remained silent and she went on, "I think I've also felt guilty masturbating while being a married woman, knowing Paul likes sex. Yet at times I felt masturbation was safer."

Her repetitive fantasy indicated why Nancy felt somewhat safer masturbating than having sex with a man. When we analyzed the fantasy, we saw that she made her male partner her enemy and pictured sex as a battle.

"When I think of the man inserting his penis in me, I can't help but feel that it's my father on top of me and in control of my life," she confessed. "He tries to do his thing while I have to lie back helplessly.

"Many times I felt that you've been doing your thing. That the analysis is all for you. Just like it's all for the man during sex. I feel you're on top of the analytic battle and enjoy curing me. I'd like to kick you in the balls for being such a big shot."

Nancy was telling me how much she resented me as a sexual and potent man. She abruptly displaced the rage as in late January 1984 she expressed renewed hatred for her husband.

I listened patiently to her complaints about Paul for several reasons. First, she was experiencing deep dissatisfaction and this had to be understood—its realistic and unrealistic causes. Second, it was becoming frightening to hate me, she was obviously running away from that hatred. At some point I would have to help her realize she viewed both Paul and me as almost the same person, which she was not ready to admit.

It was easier for Nancy to hate Paul than to despise me. The part of Nancy that hoped and believed I would be her savior, her god, her Prince Charming, caused her to idealize and idolize me. Those times I would not gratify a childish wish, she spewed fury and hate. But where there is hope, anger recedes. The more she could accept me as analyst, rather than mother, father or savior, the more she could see me as similar to Paul rather than different from him.

Behind every chronic marital complaint lies a strong unconscious wish. This is difficult for most people to accept and not too well understood by a number of psychotherapists.

The man who complains his wife is a cold, frigid bitch unconsciously wants such a woman. A warm, sexual woman would frighten him, stir up childhood sexual fantasies toward his mother he would rather suppress.

Similarly, a wife who chronically complains her husband is weak and passive unconsciously wants such a man because a potent, sexually active man would stir her childhood yearnings for her father and/or her competition with the man.

If therapist and patient form a love relationship and are mutually critical of the patient's sexual partner, the patient's complaints will be sustained. His neurosis remains unresolved and he will have neither a good marriage or a good analysis.

As I listened to Nancy's complaints about Paul, I told myself that what she complained about wanting from Paul, she was in fact wanting from me.

"He's such an exhibitionist," she said of her husband.

"He's always trying to make a point. He's rarely interested in anything but his advertising agency. He's seldom tender or warm though he always wants sex. He's one big prick who imposes himself on me all the time."

I thought of her words, "One big prick." I told her, "This is what you unconsciously want—one big prick."

As often happens in analysis, my interpretation seemed imposed to Nancy. "There you go again," she said, "trying to show off how much you know, always trying to put me down. You're one big prick, just like Paul."

Paul and I were experienced by her as narcissistic men exhibiting ourselves for our own gratification as we exploited her. When a patient is describing the throes of hatred, it is difficult for him to recognize this hatred as displacement of feelings stimulated far earlier in life. With Nancy, it was her beloved-hated father she really wanted to castigate.

Just as I had to wait until she was ready to accept the fact she had fantasies of divorcing her husband because she wanted to "divorce" me—quit therapy—I also had to wait until she was ready to accept the fact underlying all her hate—she was carrying on her lifelong battle with her mother and father, at this stage in analysis primarily with her father.

In late February 1984 as Nancy vacillated between divorcing her "narcissistic" husband or terminating analysis with her "narcissistic" analyst, believing both exploited her, I finally asked, "Do you have any thoughts why you've spent so much time and energy with two men you experience as exploitative?"

She said in an angry voice, "*All* men are exploitative, narcissistic pricks who want to use women for their own egos.

All my life I've felt it's been a man's world. And you, Freudian nitwit, ascribe the whole thing to 'penis envy.' You stupid Freudians never take culture into account but call everything penis envy. You should walk down Broadway carrying signs, 'All I believe in is penis envy.' "

She spent several sessions eloquently and accurately talking about how women have been an oppressed minority throughout the history of civilization. Her charges were valid, her indignation righteous. This is always a difficult time in analysis. The patient's accusations are true, even marital complaints have some validity. But the analyst knows the latter are used in the service of sustaining a sadomasochistic orgy, as Nancy showed for many years in her masturbation fantasy, which included murderous wishes.

Nancy saw sex as a battle, I knew that much of the screaming that emanated from the couch was sexually satisfying. I kept quiet wanting to hear where her associations would take her.

One day in April Nancy's rage focused on the hated summer vacation. She told me, "Those damned vacations of yours always stir up my anger. You're a selfish monster."

And at last she could say, "That selfishness you and Paul show is just like my egotistical father. I remember at his funeral a part of me wanted to blurt out, 'I don't think he's as great as you all think.' "

Then she turned on me. "And when I hear people talking about you and your books and other achievements, I feel like saying the same thing."

Silence for a moment, then: "And, since I'm confessing today, I feel like telling my daughter, when she speaks of her father as so marvelous, 'He's not that wonderful, Sheila. You're exaggerating his good points.' "

She went on, now in expansive mood, "I'm starting to remember something you once said to me. Do you recall saying, referring to the penis, 'You make it so important and so essential'?"

I did not answer and she continued, "I guess I do because I assume men have the kind of life I've always wanted and this makes me feel deprived. A man is the supreme being I've always wanted to be. Men get all the love and recognition. You know, it's only now, since I've been coming here that I can honestly say, 'Men have their problems too. Men have their vulnerabilities.' " She added sarcastically, "Even Herb Strean must feel sad or upset once in a while."

Nancy then talked about what Freud said kept people in analysis a long time. He believed every patient wishes to be an omnipotent child and live in Paradise—or, as Freud put it, experience life as dominated by the "pleasure principle," which excludes the "reality principle."

Nancy grew up feeling life as a woman could lead, as it did with her mother, only to disaster and death. Her envy of men, the survivors, became so intense she projected on them the murderous rage that inevitably shadowed her fear of all men to whom she felt close—her father, her brother, her husband, her principal and now me.

Life on the couch is not as dramatic as a novel or film. Inner emotional change takes place slowly and often routinely. Rewards of work on the part of both analyst and patient lie in an earthworm-paced movement in the unseen process achieved in the understanding of the self. Much takes place in the unconscious, of which the patient is unaware. The analyst senses the changes, knows that minute though they appear, in the long run they are gargantuan.

I was aware change had taken place within Nancy when one day she told me what happened the night before with Paul. She said, "After Sheila went to bed, we sat in the living room and looked out at the East River and the twinkling lights in Brooklyn. Suddenly I thought this would be a good time to initiate making love, something I had not done in years.

"I bent over to kiss Paul and thought how handsome he appeared and how sexy he really is. I also became aware how much hate I had discharged on the couch so I could feel loving and excited.

"It was fun undressing Paul and letting him undress me. While the passion we both felt was gratifying, I think what I truly enjoyed was realizing that much of the poisonous hatred I had felt over the years was draining out of my system."

She was silent a few moments, then went on, "It was as if the hundreds of analytic hours had enabled me to feel that a man was no longer my enemy—and a penis was not a hurtful instrument.

"I always used to think Paul's premature ejaculations were his problem. But now I realize I can help him feel stronger and more loving. It seems that when a woman desires a man, he feels more wanted and more potent."

She summed up, "I think that for the first time in my life, sexual passion and tenderness came together as Paul and I felt more together. It was like the first time we made love but one hundred times better because we felt more sure of ourselves and each other."

It would take time but, as she accepted her new, more mature feelings, her fear would diminish, she could feel loved by and love her husband and, most important, accept herself as a woman. She would become aware she did not have to follow in her mother's tragic footsteps. She did not have to die at an early age, she could live on, enjoy life.

We now entered the spring of her fifth year with me. I felt she had come a long way from the woman who first walked into my office with demands no one could meet. I had no doubt the year ahead would bring her nearer and nearer to what we call "sanity"—a state of mind no one enjoys completely, given what Freud called "the human condition."

P A R

T V

THE
FIFTH
YEAR

SPRING
1984

11
THE
COURAGE
TO GO IT
ALONE

May 1984
to July 1985

As the 1984 summer vacation approached, I realized how different Nancy was from the day she first walked into my office. The progress she had made seemed remarkable for someone with her emotionally disturbed history.

The first August I left her, after treating her only four months, I feared she might do something impulsive, such as commit suicide and, indeed, she did wound herself with a knife though not severely.

At that time she was very paranoid, most demanding, used poor judgment and her relationship with husband and daughter was not too happy. She had few close friends and suffered from occasional persecution delusions, focused on the principal of the school. All of us fantasize but we know the mental pictures in large part come from our imagination, we do not lose sight of reality.

At first Nancy went from fantasying to hallucinating. She occasionally said she wished I were asleep so I could not hear her forbidden desires. At other times, she really believed I fell asleep, did not recognize this as severe distortion on her part.

When I compared my countertransference reactions to Nancy—how what she said affected my thoughts and emotions—from the first summer vacation to the 1984 break, I now felt very differently about her. In the summer of 1980, I experienced myself as an extremely overanxious parent, terrified my daughter would destroy herself or try to destroy me.

At that time I felt angry, then pensive as I questioned my own judgment. I wondered if perhaps Nancy was too much for me despite the fact I had treated other schizophrenic patients. But now, in the summer of 1984, I felt warmly toward her, experienced her as a friend in many ways, a partner in a gratifying adventure and a woman who stimulated me intellectually and emotionally.

Early in my analytic training I learned that a valid way to assess a patient's progress or lack of progress is to trust your own subjective feelings toward and fantasies about the patient. You know a patient has made progress when you feel toward him as if he were a close colleague, a member of your family, a possible spouse or lover, as well as a good friend.

While a host of factors contribute to an analyst's state of mind toward the patient, such as the analyst's current life, unresolved internal and external problems and personal analysis, I believe the analyst's subjective reactions can be an excellent barometer of how well the patient progresses.

Because I felt so consistently positive toward Nancy— seeing her more and more as a mature friend and colleague and less and less as an irritating, demanding little girl—it did not surprise me in early September 1984 to hear her say, as she returned to my office, that her summer was, in many ways, enjoyable.

In her first few sessions she referred to experiencing a different image of herself. She described in detail how her life had changed, why it became more pleasurable.

"I enjoy living these days," she said. "Paul and I get along well. I have few complaints about him. Sheila is fun to be with. I realize she is a person in her own right. I no longer feel the principal is after me but on my side. On the whole I like how my life has turned out."

She added, "I think the main reason is because I no longer have to be a superman to believe I have an identity. And when I don't have to be Superman, I don't feel I am a helpless little girl."

As Nancy talked of new feelings I remembered Freud's paper "Analysis Terminable and Interminable." I thought particularly of his comment that what keeps people in analysis for many years is their strong wish to remain an omnipotent child.

All of us cling to the fantasy of having perfect parents, who love us every minute of the day and night, as we romp in the garden of Eden. While this fantasy can have different expressions, such as wanting the perfect mate or lover, hoping to make a million in the lottery, writing a best-seller, in the final analysis, Freud said, we all aspire to be the kind of superman Nancy wished to be—omnipotent and powerful.

Or, if this does not seem possible, then we want to be the child with omnipotent parents. Most of us go back and forth, trying to be omnipotent or hoping for an omnipotent partner when we marry.

In analysis when the patient aspires less and less to be a superman or demand perfect parents, we know he faces reality to a greater degree. He accepts life as it is, rather than continue to live in what Selma H. Fraiberg called, in her book of the same title, *The Magic Years*.

Fraiberg explains that in normal development, dangers both real and imaginary present themselves to the small child and if he does not acquire the means to deal with them, he is reduced to chronic helplessness and panic. This is how Nancy felt at times with her very ill mother and then at her mother's death.

According to Freud, the essential foundations of our character are set by age three. What we learn and think and feel from then on may modify but not alter the traits earlier established. Nancy somehow along the way developed a courage that drove her to analysis to try to understand why she felt so fearful and angry. For this, I admired her. It is the strong, not the weak, who seek help when they feel emotionally troubled.

As Fraiberg points out, long before a child builds inner resources for overcoming dangers, he is dependent upon his mother and father to satisfy his needs, relieve him of fear, anxiety and tension. To the infant and young child, his parents are powerful, magical creatures who automatically know his every wish, satisfy his deepest longings and perform miraculous feats without a word spoken.

When one parent disappears early in life, as in Nancy's case, the child will feel helpless, but then, if he has enough emotional strength, try to find ways to develop his own power. Nancy, we may assume, would not have had to fight so hard if her father had remarried an understanding, thoughtful woman who would have served to help Nancy mature gradually. But her father had not been emotionally capable of taking this step. For whatever reasons, he decided to be the lone parent of his daughter and son.

Nancy created her own inner world of homicidal monsters to combat the early dangers. Because, out of her childish sense of omnipotence, she believed she had killed her mother, she felt she deserved death. In a way, she constantly sought death, at least the death of her free spirit.

Yet part of her wanted to understand why she felt so terrified and angry. By seeking psychoanalytic help, she moved toward accepting life as it was, of becoming far less dominated by unrealistic wishes and impossible demands. I thought she was now well on the road to understanding her fears and fantasies.

I wondered whether it would be Nancy or me who would

broach the idea of ending the analysis—what analysts call "termination," which may take anywhere from six months to a year.

Analysts seldom consider the criteria for ending an analysis successfully. Freud wrote that the patient now should be able to enjoy "work and love." Most analysts would agree that Freud placed his "work" life ahead of his "love" life, toiling on his writings at night long after his wife went to bed.

Work and love seemed to progress fairly well for Nancy these days but was that enough to determine whether her analysis was approaching a successful end? Freud never answered that question for the generations of analysts who followed him. Though analysts after Freud who dealt with termination, such as Dr. Herman Nunberg, pointed out that a patient was ready to leave the couch when "the unconscious became conscious"—again, a rather vague criterion.

By making the unconscious conscious, Nunberg and other analysts meant that those forbidden wishes and unnecessary taboos, what analysts call "maladaptive defenses," become conscious and mental energy previously used to repress the taboo thoughts, feelings and memories may now be used for more productive work and happier relationships.

Many of Nancy's tabooed unconscious thoughts had become conscious. Forbidden, murderous fantasies, subjected to the light of reason, were now under conscious control. Her incestuous fantasies were far less terrifying, she no longer needed to deny them but could accept them as natural to we human beings. Her wish to be a man—a persistent struggle in her attempt to save her sanity as a child, as she visualized herself as Superman—had weakened. She started to accept herself as a woman, a troubled woman but a woman nonetheless.

I must confess that every time termination arose in my work, I went through the mental gymnastics I faced with Nancy. I could tell myself once again that the criteria for termination are far from exact. Like many things in psychoanalysis, the analyst's own subjective beliefs are crucial.

Dr. Stephen Firestein, author of *Termination in Analysis*, one of the few books to consider this topic, wrote that the analyst and patient often have to be satisfied with incomplete results. (Are there any complete ones? Does not the process of psychoanalysis continue until our death as we search deeper and deeper into the causes of our conflicts?)

Freud spoke of these "incomplete results," and how analyst and patient often have to accept them. Freud meant that some patients are left with a phobia, compulsion or other maladaptive distress.

I asked myself, What is incomplete about my work with Nancy?—and came to a curious but helpful conclusion.

I had to admit that in contrast to almost any other analysis I had conducted—including my own personal analysis —termination with Nancy was like a phobic issue that had never been faced or discussed by either patient or analyst. Most patients from time to time wonder about and give their thoughts on what life will be like after analysis.

Nancy and I, on the other hand, seemed to have been

playing out a drama in which we would be the Ruth and Naomi of her dreams. And, as I considered this serious omission, I came up with many pertinent answers.

First, and perhaps most important, Nancy had suffered her mother's early death—undoubtedly the most traumatic event of her life. This tragedy perplexed her as a little girl. It came close to destroying her mentally.

Second, though her father did not die until she was an adult, in many ways he failed to be a responsible, sensitive, protective, understanding father. He left Nancy on her own as a child, forced her to become a young woman far too early in life. In his fantasy she became the wife he lost, for he never sought a replacement, which affected her fantasies during the oedipal period and thereafter. That Nancy could marry and bear a child of her own was to her great credit.

Third, Nancy's brother did not champion her but made her feel challenged. He became much more a foe than a friend. He was younger and his life also was difficult, for he had a mother even fewer years than Nancy. We can only assume he received greater strength from his father, who did not have to fear his own and his daughter's oedipal desire, which would create deep guilt.

Nancy also had felt uncomfortable in her marriage to Paul but was slowly accepting him as a human being, entitled to his fears and conflicts. She had recently told me she felt far less need to masturbate as her wish for sex with Paul increased. This indeed was giving up a childhood compulsion.

Nancy had many reasons why she never mentioned terminating our relationship. I reminded myself that in essence I had become her mother, father, brother and, to some extent, lover and husband. I was also always there as the object of her anger who would not strike back. There was little reason to want to give me up. The relationship, in many ways, was too fulfilling.

Psychoanalysts have not sufficiently considered those analytic relationships that may be "too fulfilling" and "too gratifying" for the patient. From time to time, particularly for patients who feel emotionally depleted, have little gratification in their day-to-day living, the analytic relationship may become a substitute for life itself. Often this is not recognized by either analyst or patient and while the analysis goes on, in many ways the patient's life stops.

Usually, if not always, when the patient wants to make the analytic relationship a substitute for a real relationship and the analyst aids and abets the patient's demand, he might do well to examine his feelings toward the patient.

I had to ask myself, How come I had not faced the idea of life without Nancy? Just as Nancy had not faced life without Dr. Strean. I realized one fantasy I had dealt with and often monitored in my work with Nancy still remained alive in my unconscious.

The "rescue" fantasy is one I had experienced particularly in work with children. I was in this instance the superman who would deliver Nancy from the tortures of her existence into a life of happiness and joy by becoming her "everything." This reflected my own unresolved omnipotence fantasy to be every person of whose love and care the child Nancy had been deprived.

What had stopped me from facing termination with Nancy was my wish to be her mother, father, brother and lover—a very tall order. Though I had faced this rescue fantasy a few times during the course of our work, the depth and strength of it had remained unconscious until now. I realized I wanted to give Nancy what I wanted from my analyst and from life—the perfect mother and father.

One of the reasons my rescue fantasies had eluded me was because I wished to continue gratifying them. Another was because throughout Nancy's years of analysis she made good therapeutic progress. Particularly for someone diagnosed as schizophrenic, her healing process was quite outstanding. It was not until I thought about our mutual resistance to termination that I really questioned myself.

Had Nancy not made progress, I would have searched my soul more carefully at an earlier date. I reminded myself that those who ardently wish to "rescue" others are crying out to the world, "*I* want to be rescued." They project this need upon others rather than consciously admit it.

If I were going to help Nancy terminate analysis successfully, we would have to face the inevitable—understand how she would feel about life without me.

Thus, in late September when Nancy presented a dream in which she said both "good-bye" and "hello" in my office, I knew it was time to bring up her ambivalence toward leaving me. I had to help her talk about termination as I silently analyzed what life without Nancy would be like.

In response to her dream, I said, "I think you have mixed feelings about staying with me and leaving me. You're saying 'good-bye' and 'hello' in the same breath."

She responded sarcastically, "I feel quite able to function without you, inasmuch as I've done so over the past summer."

Then added in softer tone, "Look how well my life is going as a whole."

She expected me to agree with her but I maintained analytic silence, wanting to give her the chance to think what life would be like separated from me.

She then sounded irritated as she said, "Look, we've been through this thing together. We're partners in a joint venture. Aren't you going to give me your opinion about my readiness to end analysis?"

I replied, "Whenever you ask for my opinion, you have feelings of your own that are difficult to express."

She sniffed, then said, once again sarcastically, "You haven't acted like a pompous ass in a long time, Strean. Why the hell do you sit there like a cold stone, emoting nothing?"

I liked her poetic simile but said not a word, wanted her to express further thoughts.

After a long silence, now well aware the first command of analysis is, "Thou shalt keep talking," Nancy remarked, "I said 'cold stone,' didn't I?" She repeated pensively the words "cold stone" several times.

Then she said, a tone of triumph, "Of course! Cold stone is what my mother's grave looks like and now my father's grave too. If you're a cold stone, you're dead—like my mother and father."

She started to sob as if her heart was breaking. When able to stop and wipe away the tears, she said, "All my life

I wanted a loving mother and father. Then you came along and became both."

She fell silent again for a moment, then said, "Do you remember when I called you 'Mummie Herby'? And when I thought you were the father who cared? Please don't take all that away from me. I need you."

I recalled how loathe I had been to give up my analyst. This is not an easy task. Most patients feel their analysis could go on until the day they die and they would still be learning more about their secret self. It takes time to realize there are some important steps that must be taken alone. Otherwise we never break free from the parental tie as the analyst remains the good and bad parent. The analyst can show the way to greater emotional freedom but we must eventually gain the strength that comes only from going it alone.

While Nancy felt abandoned, then indignant at my suggestion of termination, I noticed she talked about her distress in a rather mature way. She was aware her anxiety over separating had much to do with her past. She was able to be more reflective about her relationship with me instead of seeing it through the eyes of a demanding, at times obstinate child.

She had become, I felt, more of a woman looking at the child in herself without now falling apart. And she felt even more reassured when I said, "Termination does not have to be abrupt. This is the fall of 1984. Perhaps we can think of actual termination as taking place at the end of 1985."

Gertrude and Rubin Blanck, authors of the two-volume *Ego Psychology, Theory and Practice*, see termination as "a process that pervades the treatment from the outset rather than as the final phase of treatment only, because the treatment process, whether psychoanalysis or psychotherapy, includes continuous promotion and ever-increasing autonomy. Ideally, by the time termination proper takes place, maximum autonomy has been attained."

The Blancks conclude, "The well-structured terminating patient experiences pain, sadness, perhaps even mourning, as has been noted in the literature." They add that termination is "appropriate when the goal of autonomous functioning has been approached."

The "goal" had certainly been approached by Nancy. No analyst expects a patient to be "cured" (though every patient expects he is going to be miraculously made perfect —the fantasy of fantasies). The word "cure" may apply to a broken leg but not to a disturbed mind.

I could, however, expect Nancy and all other successful patients to have received from therapy a new way of thinking about their lives based on the psychoanalytic "process." The psychoanalytic way of thinking—of knowing how to reach unconscious fantasies, wishes and fears—can now be used by the patient as he continues exploring his memories, fears, rages and their often unreal causes.

He will continue interpreting the meaning of his dreams as he, alone, free-associates to their words and pictures. He will think more deeply about anything that troubles him. He has discovered, through analysis, that he no longer has to act compulsively but has options in making a considered, mature decision.

The patient ready to terminate has learned to think in

a new way about "love." He now understands mature love is
not the passionate, romantic feeling that led him into an
unhappy marriage. Love is the result of a process that starts
in infancy with the tender touch of a mother and father. It
continues through childhood and adolescence as we inter-
nalize subtle facets of caring and nurturing. A sudden sexual
desire for someone new is not "love."

To love in a mature way you have to know yourself fairly
well so your demands both on yourself and the other person
are not outrageous, unrealistic ones stemming from childhood.

Psychiatrist Dr. W. Hugh Missildine points out in *Your
Inner Child of the Past* that when two persons marry they fall
"in love," physically attracted to each other. But love also
means two "children of the past" see in the other adult the
"promise of fulfillment of past longings."

After the marriage, on knowing the other better, they
come face to face with each other's "child of the past"—the
"childish" part of the spouse that seems unreasonable, demanding and hateful.

Missildine suggests "many marital difficulties and in-
compatibilities might be avoided—or at least foreseen—if
the prospective bride and groom visited one another's homes
casually and observed the relationship between the 'intended'
and his parents. The way he looks at his parents will be the
coloration through which he will see his spouse. One must
ask: 'Do I want to be treated as he treats his parents?' And
the way his parents treat him will be a good indication of how
he will treat himself and how he will expect you to behave
toward him—after the honeymoon."

The happiness of the marriage will depend on how well

"*each* of the four—the two adults and the 'inner child of the past' of each adult—can adjust on a basis of mutual respect for the other three."

Because four persons are involved, a balanced state of mutual respect is seldom achieved easily, Misseldine warns. He suggests every married person gain awareness of his marital difficulties by recognizing the part played by his "inner child of the past." He has to realize there are certain areas where he and his marital partner will differ widely. Such differences are natural to some extent, have to be accepted if the marriage is to succeed.

He also explains that emotionally "we grow like the layers of an onion." He quotes Walt Whitman as saying each day "becomes part" of us, that "the struggles and longings of our childhood and adolescence will always remain deep within us."

"It takes time to get used to the idea that these old feelings and struggles are not 'over and done with' and that the core of childhood lives on, exerting its influence," Misseldine explains. "Most of us never emotionally accept this fact. We seek to stifle or root out this part of ourselves. It is unwelcome because it doesn't confirm our adult view of ourselves."

Nancy had been helped to understand her childhood had played a vital part in shaping her acts and feelings. She had slowly accepted this as we worked hard to expose and explore the meaning of the tragedies, some overt, some subtle, in her life. She had denied them at first, wishing to be unaware of them because they had been so traumatic. As a result, her defenses had been as strong as the rock of Gibraltar. In a way we might think of the psychoanalytic process as chipping away slowly at the rock of our defenses, helping us understand our resistances to knowing the truth so that eventually we are able to face that painful truth and know in so doing we ease our suffering.

The child automatically consigns to his unconscious anything that pains him, demeans him, arouses his fear. He learns to please his parents at the cost of harming his reason, as Nancy had done. To please her father after her mother died she had to bury in her unconscious all her deepest fears and act like a well-behaved little girl. This, in the long run, had proved too overwhelming and her rebellion had manifested itself in a fiery rage against those she saw as dictators. They were the strong survivors, she was the victim.

A powerful example, somewhat similar to Nancy's, is reported in the article "The Night of the Living Dead," by Dr. Vamik D. Volkan, the famous psychoanalyst and author of many books, including *The Need to Have Enemies and Allies*. He is director of the Center for the Study of Mind and Human Interaction of the University of Virginia's Health Sciences Center and professor of psychiatry there. He has also worked to promote closer relationship between Soviet and American psychiatrists.

In his article Volkan describes his treatment of a young woman in her mid-twenties who told him she communicated with "good" and "bad" spirits from another world and felt herself to be "half woman, half man," much as Nancy did.

She had been adopted into a family to replace her adoptive mother's brother, a pilot shot down in combat. She was the only child and, Volkan explains, "analysis revealed how the way she was regarded by important others in her early environment as a living link to the dead man passed into the self-concept of the little girl, where the little girl concept could not be integrated with the dead man concept."

The paper's title, "The Night of the Living Dead," came from a film in which the dead ate the living in order to survive. Analysis showed how as a little girl, her adoptive mother and grandmother's ongoing worship of the dead pilot had given her the message she must be like him and emotionally incorporate (take within as though eating) his masculine qualities. He was the hero of her childhood—the dead pilot—and to be a worthy adopted child, she had to be like him, at least "half a man."

Nancy held this fantasy too, although it was based not on a dead man but the very alive two men in her life as she grew up. To her, to be a woman meant dying early—men were the survivors. Each person's life holds many wishes, many complexities, many opposing thoughts and feelings. When a person, as they say, "loses contact with reality," the therapist must search and search to draw out the fantasies, yearnings and hurts of childhood that have interfered with the normal process of maturation.

Nancy, like all schizophrenic patients, had been deeply depressed when she first came to me. As the story of her life unreeled in my office, I understood the frightening roots of her depression, helped her face them. Depression starts in the very early years when the child feels uncared for by a parent or in some way unloved or abused.

We now know that the causes of schizophrenia lie in an emotionally hurtful childhood. The schizophrenic patient, like the neurotic patient, must become aware of his hurt and the defenses he used to protect against it—depression, denial, the overuse of fantasy to blot out cruel reality.

The patient slowly acquires the capacity for self-analysis, following the thinking of the analyst. This self-analysis brings him new strength, one that permits him to separate from the analyst and continue using on his own the newly acquired insights.

Nancy was now able to rely on herself to a far greater degree than in the past. In the safe harbor of the analytic room she could speak of her depression, her rage, her fears and, unlike her childhood parents, I would not reproach her, hate her, wish she would disappear. Like every patient, Nancy had hoped to be magically "cured" of whatever conflicts had caused her unhappiness over the years.

I could feel I helped her transform what Freud called "hysterical misery" into "common unhappiness." Complete happiness is pure fantasy. There are always conflicts to be solved but as Nancy's misery eased, her conflicts did not seem as threatening or as unsolvable. Her improved relationship with her husband showed that, as well as her acceptance of those she formerly saw as enemies.

She was now capable of being more of a nurturing wife and mother. Her ability to nurture anyone had been very low, for she had received little nurturing in life. We learn how to nurture by being nurtured. My concern for her, which she felt, my understanding of her painful past, my wish she understand and recover slowly from it, all helped bring out her nurturing qualities. She was now far more caring toward her husband and daughter.

Throughout the analysis, no sooner did I think Nancy was making substantial and permanent gains but she would take a psychic step backward. Most analytic experiences are reflected in the termination phase and Nancy showed me once again how easy it was to regress.

In late November 1984, after we discussed the possibility of Nancy living without formal analysis, she developed a symptom only present once or twice during the analysis though it appeared on and off from childhood until she entered analysis. She started to suffer profound asthmatic attacks.

She said apologetically, "I've had these attacks before, as you know. They're the pits."

Nancy used the word "pits" several times. I sensed there was a connection between "pits" and her asthma attacks. I said, "When you talk about your asthma, several times now you've used the word 'pits.' What are your associations to 'pits'?"

After a short silence Nancy started to sob. Then, wiping away her tears, she blurted out, "Snake pits. The goddamned mental hospitals. I haven't thought about them in a long time. But they were the places I suffered from asthma most often. I kept wheezing and wheezing, as if calling out for somebody to take care of me, mother me."

Nancy gave me probably the best verification of psychoanalytic thought about asthma. It represents a crying-out for a mother expressed through the body. The child feels that direct expression of desire for the mother is useless—it will not bring the response he yearns for and needs. So the child holds back his wishes but unconsciously they appear through the asthma attack, as if to say, "I'm falling apart. Come hold me. Come take care of me."

Nancy's asthma attacks at this final phase of analysis bore a very important message. It was as if she once more had to squelch her yearning for a mother but did not dare say directly what she felt.

I commented one day in December 1984, as the attacks continued, "The idea of ending analysis is like giving up mother. You apparently are finding it very difficult to tell me you still want me as a mother. You are also finding it difficult to tell me how angry you are at ending the analysis."

Nancy did not need too much encouragement to reveal how she felt at this point. She reverted to the anger she needed desperately to express, hurled at me: "Yes, you goddamned bastard. Like both of my parents, you're forcing me to become an adult too swiftly. You don't even know how to do psychoanalysis correctly. You know I shouldn't be forced to grow up so quickly. But that's what you're doing to me. All my life I've needed support and contact and reassurance and you're taking it all away. You say to me, 'Get lost, you lousy kid.' And I wonder what it is you hate about me that's making you say, 'Beat it, I hate you.' "

She fell into silence, I waited her out. Finally she said, in calmer tone, "What you're doing right now makes me feel like I did when I went to the snake pits. Hated. Rejected. Punished. Just as the mental hospitals appeared hopeful on the outside but miserable on the inside, this is how you seem to me."

The tears started to flow again. Nancy felt hated by me

at this point, rejected, misunderstood. Like the doctors at the mental hospitals, who gave her a cursory examination, then arranged for electroshock treatment, she felt I had proposed termination too quickly—as if I were administering psychic shock treatment.

She accused, "I can't tell if I'm talking to you or the goddamned hospital psychiatrists who showed no compassion but tortured me further. I was only a zombie to them."

Just as Nancy reacted to the shock treatment with bizarre giddiness and inappropriate laughter, she now behaved similarly with me. And just as she screamed during the acute phases of her psychosis, she screamed from the couch during some of her sessions in December 1984, and the first month of 1985.

"Don't do this to me!" she would loudly entreat. "Be my Mummy Herby. Don't forsake me or I will die. Why are you punishing me by making me leave you?"

As she showed her anguish I felt mixed emotions. On the one hand perhaps she was right, I was therapeutically overambitious, too premature in believing she could manage by herself. Though I told myself that—as was true with any patient with whom I worked—she could always return for more treatment, I felt like a selfish parent who asked more than a child was able to give.

Yet I also knew Nancy needed to talk at length of her feelings regarding the separation. She had to understand why and how she always distorted autonomy and independence. She believed every time she was on her own she was being punished for some evil deed.

I let her once again pour out her hatred toward me

for being the cruel and insensitive mother and father she felt I was. If she did not improve in her functioning and in her ability to cope with her feelings, we could always postpone the termination date. It was not a magical day.

Nancy continued to associate to her experiences in the mental hospitals. One day in early March she revealed, "Each time I suffered insulin or electroshock treatments, I thought I was getting rid of devils, receiving punishment I deserved."

I asked, "Why do you need to be punished? You view the mental hospital as a place to be punished and now you see termination of analysis as punishment."

She answered at once, "If you loved me, you'd hold onto me. There's something about me that's bad, that you don't like and I am being punished for it."

"What is it you think I don't like?"

After quiet reflection she said slowly, "I guess I haven't made peace with the feeling—it's still more like a fact—that I killed my mother. I was furious because she wasn't really there when I needed her as a little girl. I couldn't understand how very ill she was. And when she died, I felt a guilt that engulfed me—a guilt I have never faced before coming here."

She continued, "And I think that throughout the analysis so much of your silence reminded me of my mother, who would not speak to me, answer my questions. This made me believe she didn't care. I don't remember her ever smiling at me. Or holding me in her arms."

She coughed, then said, "All the devils in me are really my hateful feelings toward my mother. And now you, for not loving me the way a child deserves to be loved."

As she discharged hatred once again, talked of her yearnings to be held and loved, the asthma attacks disappeared. Her agitation also diminished to a large extent.

In late March she told me how she managed to get out of one mental hospital "by acting better but feeling worse," after five months (her stays were shorter in the other four hospitals). She was informing me I was asking her to "act better" even though she felt "worse."

She started to contrast her analytic experience with that in the mental hospitals. She said, "I realized that the thing I dreaded most was that there was no one I could really talk to. Every time I wanted to say something I thought important, the message I got in one way or another was 'Shut up!' I felt the best way to get along was to keep my mouth closed. My rage mounted and I had no way to express it."

She let out a short, sarcastic laugh. "Sometimes I would look in the mirror to see if I was human. I'd prick my skin to see if I reacted like a normal person."

Her tone changed to a more sympathetic one. "But psychoanalysis is very different. I am allowed to talk, I am even urged to talk, sometimes I feel I talk too much. And you are different, very different, from those doctors in their white jackets. Anything I say is acceptable to you. You never judge. And without realizing it I no longer judge myself so harshly because I've learned from you that anything I feel is okay. It doesn't hurt anyone else."

I now felt Nancy was far less melancholic, though obviously in mourning. At this time she seemed not so tormented by guilt, less agitated, but quite genuinely sad. I thought of

Freud's paper "Mourning and Melancholia," in which he pointed out that when someone dies and we essentially love him, hold only limited hatred toward him, we mourn and feel sad but recover within a few months.

But in melancholia, when we feel more hate than love, we are apt to become deeply agitated and full of self-hatred. We believe that our hatred, almost always accompanied by the wish to kill, has caused the person's death.

Nancy was feeling less melancholia because she had now been able to express and thus master much of her early hatred toward her mother by first venting it at me. She could identify with my nonpunitive and nonjudgmental approach. She loved herself more, punished herself less. Like any mature person who enjoyed a close relationship with a parent, she could genuinely mourn the loss of her mother and the approaching loss of my presence four afternoons a week.

Nancy's need to scream at me occasionally was the anger of a child weaned prematurely, toilet-trained far too early and made to fend for herself too soon in life. When she could understand that she might hate me, placing me in the role of her parents, and blame me for all her destructive feelings, her anger and misery receded.

I gave her the right to release her long-buried anger. Anger from a time she had every right to be furious. She as a hurt child had faced a dying mother, did not understand her own or her mother's acute misery.

In early April 1985 Nancy brought up another theme that frequently occurred during her analysis, bound to reemerge during termination. As she started to accept analysis as a "successful achievement," some of her guilt feelings that we had analyzed carefully connected to achievements, emerged once again—one of the ways patients hope to ward off termination is to regress.

She said, "I'm beginning to feel superior to too many people. My father, my mother, my brother, even Paul at times. And toward all the people who've never been analyzed, who don't have my insights and the capacity to enjoy life as much as I now do."

I asked, "What bothers you about being superior and feeling superior?"

She said thoughtfully, "I never believed you would think in those terms. I thought everybody except God and the analyst is supposed to be equal. And now you're saying that it's okay to feel better, stronger, more capable than other people?"

I did not answer her question. Without censuring me as she often did when I remained silent, she said with glee, "I know what you're trying to tell me. You're trying to say that every time I felt superior to somebody in the past, I was trying to show them up, demean them and derogate them. And then I hated myself for feeling so contemptuous, followed, as the day the night, by guilt."

I still said nothing, she went on, "I'm really integrating what I think one of the greatest gifts I've received from analysis. *The right to achieve. The right to feel superior.* I no longer have to turn life into a fight. I can know I am better than some people but don't have to laugh at them as if they were my mother, father, brother or someone on whom I was seeking revenge for past hurts."

Nancy had indeed learned one of the major lessons psychoanalysis can provide—you can achieve, you can enjoy a better life than your parents or siblings, you can feel and be superior at times without feeling guilt or remorse.

We feel guilt and remorse, then expect punishment, only when we carry out what are usually unconscious battles whose purpose is to hurt or demean others as we move ahead. You do not have to preen like a peacock when you achieve an honor you deserve. You can instead quietly accept the achievement and move on from there.

I also explained to Nancy, hoping to lessen her fear of leaving analysis, "There is no such thing as ending an analysis. It will go on and on inside you the rest of your life. You can analyze your own dreams, as you do much of the time here. You are a very bright, sensitive woman and can think through many of your deeper conflicts."

She put in hastily, "And I've learned a new way of thinking about those conflicts because of your help. I'm very grateful for that."

Although I reassured Nancy a few times there was no rule about how long an analysis takes, no rule about ending on a specific date (and there was always the possibility she could return for a few sessions), she told me in late April, "I think I would like to consider termination when you go on your vacation." This would be the summer of 1985.

I told her I would respect her wishes, but we should continue to evaluate what happened in her life and in the analysis between now and the end of July. She agreed, saying, "I know how important this will be."

She spent the last months talking mainly about how much she would miss me. In many ways I represented the mother and father she wanted to live with, the brother to whom she wished to feel close, the lover she felt would make life exciting.

The more she talked of her fantasies of living with me, where she could be at times the child, the wife, the lover, the sister, the more she could also acknowledge this would never be. Though such deprivation was difficult to accept, she now knew it would be unrealistic to keep chasing this psychic rainbow. She was giving up more and more what Freud called the "wish to be omnipotent" as well as the wish to possess an omnipotent parent.

In our last session at the end of July, she started off by saying, "I know this is our final session, but I also know I will want to see you again. This to me is very reassuring because it takes care of so many of the fears I've had all my life. I can say good-bye and know I am not killing you or angering you. This is a new, wonderful feeling to realize my strength does not weaken you or any other soul."

Then she said, "This is a sad day but far from the saddest. I feel like a beloved child going off to college but leaving a happy home. It's upsetting but not so much that I can't handle it. I feel alone but not lonely."

I felt much of the same sadness as I recalled the many separations in my own life. Like Nancy, I was often very angry because of premature and unwanted separations. And, like Nancy, I was feeling sad at her termination, clearly mourning the loss of someone who had become for me the daughter I never had, the sister who had left me for another man when she married. It was as though Nancy were a unique, special friend.

I listened to Nancy's expressions of profound melancholia and praise of analysis, felt some sadness as well as pleasure as I anticipated the end of our relationship, reflected on our mutually constructive work.

Toward the end of this last session I thought of Theodor Reik's description of his final encounter with his mentor, Sigmund Freud. Reik, in *Listening with the Third Ear*, wrote in a poignant epilogue titled "Leave-taking," that "after we shook hands I stood at the door and could not say a word. My lips were pressed together so hard that they were unable to part. He must have sensed what I felt: he put his arms on my shoulders and said, 'I've always liked you.' As I bowed my head, wordless, he said in a low but firm voice as if to comfort me, 'People need not be glued together when they belong together.' "

I did not say to Nancy what Freud had said to Reik but I felt precisely what Freud felt and put into words. I comforted myself many times during vulnerable leave-takings with the thought, "People need not be glued together when they belong together."

Analysts and patients feel somewhat emotionally bonded during treatment, and forever after remain glued to a certain degree in memory. It is this feeling of closeness, reflecting a time during which so much is experienced by each, that enables the patient to continue analysis alone.

EPILOGUE: MORE HUMAN THAN OTHERWISE

1985

In the five years since I ended the treatment of Nancy W., she has been in touch with me on four different occasions. I assured her she could call for a consultation if she felt troubled. This meant she would sit in the chair opposite me, no longer on the couch.

The first time she appeared she told me, "I'm concerned because Sheila seems mildly depressed. I need advice on how to help her."

The rest of her life, she said, seemed to be proceeding fairly smoothly. She was coping well with marriage, work, relationships with friends.

Early in the practice of psychoanalysis I became aware of a principle I always found helpful as I listen to parents talk of their children's conflicts. Whenever a parent speaks of a child's problem, this is really a revelation of how the parent feels. The mother or father who says, "My child needs information about sex," invariably requests the information for himself.

Similarly, the mother or father who says, "My youngster does not respond to limits," is telling his listener he has difficulty responding to limits. Thus, when Nancy informed me Sheila was "mildly depressed," I said to myself, Something is depressing Nancy.

I also learned that as you talk to the parent about a child, his description of the youngster is a description of the parent himself. Children unconsciously copy the parent, carry out the parent's wishes.

Consequently, I asked Nancy, "What do you suppose is depressing Sheila these days?"

She replied, tears in her eyes, "I think Sheila is lonely. She seems to want to be more attached to somebody."

I asked, "How long has Sheila been lonely and looking for an attachment?"

She wiped the tears away with a tissue, said, "Several months."

"What during these several months brought on Sheila's loneliness?"

Nancy asked, "Do you think I'm projecting something onto Sheila?" Her eyes held a look of wonder.

I asked, "Do you?"

She looked at me, a half-smile on her attractive face, said, "I'm lonely for you. I miss you. For five years and four months I enjoyed a unique experience talking to you four times a week, saying everything that came to my mind. You were always there for me."

She took a deep breath, went on, "Though I feel pretty good about myself today, my life is not quite the same without you. I am forced to be more independent than I really want to be. I still feel so *damned* alone."

"In the long run we are all alone," I said. "We have to become aware we can depend only on ourselves to direct our lives. Analysis can set the path but the patient then must continue down it alone, knowing it is a smoother path than the one he had to traverse before analysis."

She said ruefully, "It isn't easy."

"It never is," I assured her. "It takes time, patience, understanding of the unconscious, to attain what someone once called the eventual supremacy of reason."

"I am aware that ending analysis stirred memories and feelings of when I was alone after my mother died," she admitted. "I have never really mourned her death. It was too traumatic for me to handle at the time."

Then added, "I'm probably unwittingly putting Sheila too much on her own. And I haven't faced the depth of the anger I feel toward you, which I realize is ancient anger toward my mother and father, who forced me to grow up prematurely."

She asked if she could return the following week for one more session. At that time she said, "I felt so much better after my consultation last week. When I got home Sheila told me, 'Mummy, you're all smiles today,' and that made me feel happy."

She spoke reflectively, pensively. "For a child to smile, she needs a mother who smiles. And for a mother to smile, she needs to have felt mothered as a child."

She sighed, went on. "Paul and I are getting along well but he's no replacement for a mother or an analyst. I cannot ask him to be the good mother and father I never had."

I thought, This is the very reason so many marriages fail. Each partner demands of the other he be the "good parent" he never experienced in childhood. This is bound to occur to some degree in marriage, for we never fully relinquish the omnipotent wishes of childhood. But if our demands are too unrealistic, no one can meet them.

I wondered if perhaps Nancy needed more analysis at this time. I asked myself, How effective has her treatment really been, has she had enough to enable her to handle daily life?

Then, at least for the time being, she allayed my doubts as she said, "I suppose I'll always to some degree wish to be mothered but just knowing I can turn to you, that you're still alive, in contrast to my mother, is very reassuring. I know you won't abandon me. And that you want the best for me."

She stood up, it was the end of the hour. She said with a dignity I had never sensed in her before, "I am going to try going it alone so I can truly be stronger. I'll let you know how it works out in a few months."

But it was not until a year later that she again sought me out. She walked into the office in a fairly happy mood. She reported, "Sheila is doing much better now. So am I. To my surprise the school offered me a supervisory position. I no longer teach but instruct others. Life seems far easier."

Her only complaint, which she expressed in a low voice, centered on Paul. "We're doing better, though I'm not as interested in him sexually as I was for some time."

Just as I learned the complaints of parents about their children are really unconscious wishes, so too I have become convinced that marital partners' complaints about each other are also unconscious wishes. The mother or father who says, "My son is too inhibited," or "My daughter is too shy," unconsciously wants an inhibited or shy child. An aggressive, outgoing child would upset them. The wife who complains her husband is too passive, unconsciously wishes a passive husband. A sexually active one would frighten her.

I thought, as Nancy spoke, What is going on within her that makes her want to inhibit herself with her husband? This complaint was not new and though she was a well-educated patient, I could not barge in with an interpretation but had to explore the issue with her to understand the demands of unconscious.

I asked, "How long have you felt this mild inhibition?"

She said, "For several months."

I wondered what was happening in her life and she promptly told me, as though reading my mind: "I enjoy sex most of the time but I still feel something is missing."

I picked up the word "missing," asked, "Missing?"

She said sadly, "I guess I still miss you."

Then she told me, "Part of me is angry that it is Paul with whom I find myself in bed rather than lying on your couch."

She suddenly became very animated, said with deep conviction, "Analysis is a crazy procedure. You get as close to another human being as you have ever been or will be. You share your most intimate secrets, discuss your most hideous terrors and leave this person forever with nothing more than a handshake."

We sat in silence for a moment. Then she went on, "I suppose I could try more analysis. But I know what you'd do. You'd want to know what I feel that makes me want you as a sexual partner. And then we'd get into wishes I've repeated over one hundred times—that I want you to be the perfect mother and father I never had."

She ended the consultation saying, "I feel a bit frustrated knowing you'll always be my analyst and nothing else, but the analysis has been so helpful and enriching that I accept you cannot help me further. That you want me to go it alone."

She added, with a half-smile, "So I'll try," as if implying she still doubted her inner strength.

Almost a year passed, then in 1986 she called me for the last time. Her life at home with husband and daughter, and at school, was "much happier," she told me, but she still wanted to see me for one final session. She assured me the insights from the last three meetings had helped her considerably.

When she arrived I noticed she looked particularly well dressed and seemed more lively than I had ever seen her. As she sat down she announced, "I didn't need any excuse to see you today. I just wanted to say hello. I don't need marital or parent-child conflicts to justify a visit. At first I felt somewhat apologetic for wanting to come back. As if it meant I was not the well-analyzed person I thought I should be. But in a way I'm proud of myself to be able to come here just to say hello."

Nancy talked in this final session more like a friend on a visit. She laughed, shed a few tears, reflected on some of my past words. She concluded the session saying, "If I feel that by seeing you once a year I am not doing anything wrong, I'll enjoy the year far more."

We shook hands as she left. I have not seen her for three years. After the fourth consultation I thought of Freud's statement that schizophrenia cannot be analyzed because of the schizophrenic's extreme "narcissism." I wondered what psychological impediment made him conclude very infantile men and women, unable to feel much self-esteem, cannot be helped therapeutically.

I speculated that perhaps Freud's "narcissism" was punctured as he tried to cope with the slow progress of very infantile patients. Freud, as an infant, was called "my golden Ziggy" by his doting mother, he always yearned to be the one and only in her life. He suffered deep resentment toward his younger siblings—one brother and five sisters. He never could accept with equanimity sharing his mother with anyone, including his father.

The schizophrenic patient is like an infant who constantly demands the attention and love of the therapist. For Freud, this probably stirred his own deep yearnings and need for attention, which he found difficult to cope with. He often used cigars to quiet his yearnings for the breast even after he knew he had cancer of the jaw. He said he did not want to give up cigars because he would then be forced to face some intense feelings for and experiences with his mother.

Like all therapists, who are indeed mortal, Freud could carry out only what he himself suggested—help the patient as far as he, the therapist, had grown in an emotional sense. I am absolutely convinced that what Freud said nearly seventy-five years ago is as true today as it was then. I am also convinced the main reason so many psychiatrists, psychoanalysts and other helping professionals do not treat the schizophrenic patient psychotherapeutically or psychoanalytically is that they do not wish to face the primitive infant within themselves.

I further believe those clinicians who have faced their powerful and primitive childish wishes and accept them as part of the human condition, think of the schizophrenic patient as a human being overwhelmed by the fears and rage of his early years.

When a therapist in his work with a patient cannot face the feelings and fantasies the patient arouses in him, he may cease treatment that relates to the exchange of what, to him, seem dangerous words and thoughts. This happened in the case of Freud's mentor, the famed Dr. Josef Breuer, who fled his patient, Anna O., when he could not tolerate his sexual feelings toward her. Anna O.'s real name, Bertha, was the same as that of Breuer's beloved mother, who died when he was a boy.

When Anna O. hallucinated a pregnancy by Breuer, he may have unconsciously felt as if he had impregnated his mother. He fled the scene, never to see Anna O. again, gave up "analyzing" patients. Freud spoke of Anna O. as the one who "led me to psychoanalysis," for she coined the phrase the "talking cure." Freud evidently could tolerate his feelings toward his mother with more equanimity than Breuer.

Therapists possess many ways to flee their own vulnerabilities as these become activated in work with patients. I believe, though many will disagree, the reason so many clinicians think biological and genetic factors are the cause of schizophrenia is because they do not wish to face the inevitable anxiety, terror and infantile wishes the schizophrenic patient induces in them.

When I taught theories of personality to doctoral students at Rutgers University, I discovered that how we conceptualize any phenomenon has a great deal to do with our personal history. Dr. Karen Horney, a well-known analyst, had a father who was a sea captain. He sometimes took her on his voyages but more frequently left her home with her mother. Horney, who felt ambivalent toward all men with whom she lived and worked, conceptualized the cause of neurosis as "loneliness in a hostile world". This was how she felt as a child when her father left her for months on end to sail the seven seas.

The personalizing in analytic theory of the trauma in early life was also evident in Dr. Alfred Adler, one of the original analysts of Freud's group. He had been a physically ill boy who suffered from rickets. Doctors predicted he would never graduate from elementary school. His major concept, as a psychoanalyst, became "organ inferiority." He also felt deep resentment toward his older brother, postulated that the "ordinal position of the sibling" was a major contribution to neurosis. Adler, a very competitive man, believed people were influenced by "how they strive for superiority."

Freud, who spent much of his early childhood sleeping in the parental bedroom, founded the oedipus complex. It arose from later facing and accepting his tabooed sexual wish to possess his mother and destroy his father. This normal desire had been enhanced by the many nights he slept in the same room as his parents, undoubtedly at times witnessing or sensing parental intercourse.

The early life of Dr. Harry Stack Sullivan, a leading American psychiatrist, was a lonely one. He grew up as a withdrawn, sensitive boy, who lived on a farm in upstate New York. He became a pioneer in the analytic treatment of schizophrenic patients, known for their lonely, withdrawn, super-sensitive qualities.

Just as leading psychoanalysts reveal themselves in their theories, I believe those clinicians who champion genetics and biology as the cause of schizophrenia tell us they do not wish to consider their own psyches or those of their patients—thus the back-ward seclusion, the electroshock, the drugs.

Nancy's therapy, I believe, inalterably reveals that the schizophrenic patient, like all humans, falls ill largely because of the uncaring, often cruel way his parents treated him. Repeatedly, I have discovered that patients like Nancy, diagnosed as schizophrenic, were severely scapegoated by extremely ambivalent parents—parents unable to give their child needed love and care because of their own tormented pasts.

The person who becomes schizophrenic never knew as

a child whether he would be loved or hated, appreciated or demeaned, neglected or paid attention to. He never had a sense of who he was or what to expect from his parents. This is why he is sometimes referred to as a "split personality," sometimes rational, sometimes quite irrational, as Nancy appeared when she started treatment in my office.

I discovered an important fantasy of the schizophrenic patient. Both therapist and layman insufficiently appreciate that the schizophrenic patient behaves in a seemingly bizarre way to avoid committing murder. Since childhood he has carried within himself a burning fury.

As noted with Nancy, the schizophrenic feels deep hatred as he lives with terrifying murderous fantasies. Rather than act out the murderous wishes, he turns them against himself. He feels as Nancy did—a monster. He starts behaving like a monster, often screaming out his wrath.

Both the actual murderer and the patient diagnosed as schizophrenic are possessed by terror. *Any one of us, given enough fear, enough stress in our souls, can become schizophrenic.* This was clearly shown in the military during the war where reasonably stable men, confronted by killing others or being killed, became so terrified and helpless they suffered hallucinations and delusions as Nancy did.

When removed from a kill-or-be-killed situation, most of the men recovered. Just as the schizophrenic patient who has lived in terror for years learns that a human relationship does not necessarily involve the potential danger of killing or being killed, he no longer needs the defense of his schizophrenic symptoms.

Sometimes, as in Nancy's case, the full-blown psychosis

with its attendant hallucinations and delusions, does not appear until the person reaches his twenties or later. But an attentive observer would have seen the signs if he had listened to Nancy's descriptions of her childhood and adolescence.

Men and women, even children at times, murder out of an abject terror that began in their earliest years. They were usually the victim of beatings or witnessed parents acting out violence against each other or siblings. The murderer, as a child, felt both terrified of his life and too weak to fight. But as an adult he has the physical strength to retaliate, unfortunately often choosing the innocent as his unconscious replacement for the earlier tormentors.

Rage is a question of degree, there is not one child, man or woman who does not to some extent hate his parents. A child's every wish, every fantasy, can never be fulfilled, but if his parents are kind to him and love him, he can learn to accept frustration without intense murderous feelings of revenge.

The schizophrenic patient, rather than act on his murderous impulses, turns them inward. He feels himself a monster, as Nancy did, starts behaving at times in monstrous ways. The killer and the schizophrenic patient are filled with terror but the murderer takes another's life, believing he rids himself of the one who caused the original terror. The schizophrenic patient tries to cope with his terror by heaping all varieties of abuse on himself. He feels the world is out to get him, as Nancy felt the principal and her colleagues were out to destroy her.

Like most schizophrenic patients, Nancy felt deeply guilt-ridden. She spent far more time talking about what a "horrible" person she was because she imagined she murdered her mother than planning any actual murder.

I believe, as I have said, parental neglect or mishandling of the child is the major cause of schizophrenia. Not out of malice but out of serious emotional problems of their own, parents of schizophrenic children place themselves and their youngsters on the kind of emotional seesaw I perceived in Nancy. I have also observed that if parents receive the help they need, they become more loving and their children are spared severe emotional problems.

Not only psychoanalysts but professionals in other areas are helping the schizophrenic patient discharged from a mental hospital or who has escaped being sent to one. Since 1948 Fountain House, a nonprofit organization, has pioneered in the development of comprehensive community-based rehabilitation programs for the mentally ill.

Fountain House, whose executive director is James R. Schmidt, is located at 425 West 47th Street in New York City, and is open 365 days a year. Its programs include a prevocational day program, transitional employment opportunities in commerce and industry, a full-time employment program, evening and weekend social and recreational programs, community housing alternatives, a subsidized food program and an education program for members.

Fundamental to the Fountain House model is the concept that those involved in its programs are "members" rather than "patients" or "clients." The basic tenet is that, given time, a productive, functioning life is a reasonable and attainable goal for every member. Fountain House serves all ethnic and racial groups. Members range in age from sixteen up. The sole source of income of nearly all members is public assistance or social security. Daily attendance currently averages over 375 members.

Fountain House has gained an international reputation as the founder of the "clubhouse model" for vocational and social rehabilitation of the mentally ill in the community. Through the Van Ameringen Center for Education and Research, established at Fountain House in 1975, and its twelve-year-old National Training Program, Fountain House has provided major leadership in establishing clubhouses throughout the country.

The National Training Program provides opportunities to community mental health centers and other facilities that serve the mentally ill. The National Institute of Mental Health, which funded the training program for ten years through 1986, has called it one of the most successful training efforts underwritten by the training branch.

Fountain House trains colleagues from all parts of the world—with 885 colleagues from 438 agencies representing the United States and Canada, Denmark, Egypt, England, Holland, South Korea, Pakistan, Poland, South Africa, Sweden and West Germany. There are more than 250 independent clubhouses around the world based on the Fountain House model. A recent three-year grant from the Robert Wood Johnson Foundation is helping to further expand and strengthen the network of clubhouses in this country.

The expansion could have a profound effect in helping to solve the problems of the deinstitutionalized and homeless mentally ill. Fountain House has shown, through the development of the clubhouse program and especially through its Transitional Employment Program, that given time and support, a significant percentage of the mentally ill can not only function in the community but maintain independent living and employment.

The "members" of clubhouse programs are engaged in a wide variety of restorative activities related to the operation of the clubhouse itself. By working alongside staff and other members, and performing needed tasks, a member achieves a sense of belonging and of having friends. Members discover that, despite a history of psychiatric hospitalization, they now feel self-worth and can look forward with hope to the future.

The clubhouse programs deal with case management and the housing, social, and educational needs of the mentally ill. The programs are not limited as to time and offer all members continued opportunities to achieve their highest possible level of functioning in the community.

To assure that its members have the opportunity to return to work, Fountain House developed, in 1957, what is now called Transitional Employment (TE). This concept is integral to the rehabilitation process, providing continuous opportunities to work on time-limited, paid, part-time jobs in commerce and industry.

TE uses entry-level positions to provide this basic work experience as members discover or rediscover their capacity to develop behaviors they must observe to be successful in such employment if they are to achieve independent employment of their own choosing.

Stephen N. Guntli, director of development, sums up:

"During our forty years of existence, Fountain House has become adept at helping members move through our programs to their highest possible level of functioning. Members and staff join in discovering that each member, however ill, is not a collection of symptoms but an individual who can help shape the world in which he lives."

Unlike those who direct activities at Fountain House, unfortunately too many clinicians falsely believe schizophrenia is a fixed state that cannot be altered. Anyone who has worked with a schizophrenic patient in therapy notes just the opposite, as I did with Nancy. Schizophrenic patients have their emotional vicissitudes, their rational and irrational moments, just like other patients.

The schizophrenic patient, like Nancy, feels he is worthless, has felt this way from childhood. No amount of reassurance, as I noted in the early work with Nancy, appears to help him feel otherwise. Only persistent, consistent caring on the part of the therapist will help him feel he is as worthy as anyone else.

Unfortunately, just as the schizophrenic patient often sensed his parents wanted to get rid of him, he finds some helping professionals respond in the same fashion. Nancy felt insecure and isolated during childhood, later the mental hospitals treated her much as her parents did. The hospitals became "snake pits," for her and all other patients, real-life incarnations of psychic and mythical monsters.

There is nothing magical or particularly unique about psychotherapy with the schizophrenic patient. As mentioned earlier, I saw it succeed to some degree when first-year social work students showed a consistently humane, persistent approach, one I advocated many years ago and still advocate.

I believe the therapist's theoretical orientation to psychotherapy with the schizophrenic patient is, however, secondary—the therapist must first be aware of his inner self, whether he is Freudian or non-Freudian, Adlerian or Sullivanian. The main issue is that he does psychotherapy in humane fashion, refrains from using the brutal procedures of electroshock, insulin, drugs and other means that have proved ineffective.

When some schizophrenic patients receive shock or other nonpsychotherapeutic forms of help, they may improve for a while. The reason may be explained psychologically. As Nancy showed me, when a patient feels deeply guilt-ridden and unconsciously seeks punishment, being subjected to electroshock will ease the guilt temporarily. So does seclusion in a back ward, much as sending a child to his room—but the results are also only temporary.

The major component in the reduction of the terror the schizophrenic has felt all his life is the attitude of the one who tries to help him reduce that terror. The therapist must see himself as similar to the patient in fears, fantasies and wishes. As he can accept *his* own childhood dependency, childhood murderous wishes and childhood sexual feelings, he can then understand them in the schizophrenic patient.

The "cure" for schizophrenia rests in the change in thinking of the many mental health professionals who deny they are quite similar to their patients. When therapists are able to acknowledge the "schizophrenia" in themselves, as I tried with all my heart to do during Nancy's treatment, the patient's schizophrenia will diminish and, hopefully, disappear.

Psychotherapists should heed Hamlet's soul-searching words: "This above all: to thine own self be true," if they wish to help the schizophrenic patient achieve what we call "normalcy."

The more emotionally disturbed a patient, the more difficult it is to help him achieve normalcy. But the reward for the analyst is equally greater for he has penetrated to a deeper degree the mysteries of the human mind—the greatest mystery of all.